Pinky

MARIA BALAIS

Archway Publishing books may be ordered through booksellers or by contacting:

Archway Publishing
1663 Liberty Drive
Bloomington, IN 47403
www.archwaypublishing.com
844-669-3957

ISBN: 978-1-4808-9678-9 (sc)
ISBN: 978-1-4808-9677-2 (hc)
ISBN: 978-1-4808-9679-6 (e)

Library of Congress Control Number: 2020918620

Print information available on the last page.

Archway Publishing rev. date: 11/28/2020

CONTENTS

DEDICATION

This book is dedicated to CJ.

ACKNOWLEDGEMENTS

Perrin Cothran Conrad, Stephe Koontz, Christopher Matos-Rogers, Keith Sagers, Reggie Peagler, Mitchell King, Mia McCaskill, Wayne Murphy, Mindy Pillow, Nedra White-Shaw, Stuart Jackson, Janice Robinson, Mark Zimmerman, Salvador Chavez-Holzman, Sean Griffith, Melissa George, Cristina Stewart, Nathaniel Smith, Sam Zamarripa, Shawn McIntosh.

PREFACE

On the Tuesday night after Thanksgiving 2019, my ex-husband, Tony, my brother in-laws, Christopher and Dee Jay, and my son were at my house for a family dinner. They were roasting a honey and orange glazed duck, making a green bean casserole, garlic mashed potatoes, a crisp salad, and Tony's father's stuffing, which the main ingredients were salt and butter. There was the glow of the Christmas tree, fresh cut flowers on the table, my mother's china, and my Christmas napkins and napkin rings. We were sipping on Great King Street scotch, and pinot grigio. Our 11 year old son, CJ, had on his headphones and was playing video games and snacking on popcorn while dinner cooked.

We were finally celebrating Thanksgiving and my adoption birthday which is December 6th. Though Tony and I have been divorced for five years, we are very amicable and committed to co-parenting our son. Naturally the subject of my book came up. I said, "I have been writing the book for two years, laying the foundation and experimenting with my voice and my words for on social media."

Tony shakes his head and said, "Nope. You have been writing this book for twenty years. When we were dating and then married, you talked about writing a book many times. It has been on your mind for as long as I have known you."

I paused and then I said, "You're right. It was like elevator music. It was present, yet in the background. Always in the background."

Since that conversation, I have deeply contemplated why the book was finally coming to fruition. One of the things that did not crystalize for me until now was the purpose for writing the book. Did I want the book to be entertaining? Sure. Did I want to talk about my mother and my family? Yes. But why? Did I have a message I wanted to deliver? Probably.

A couple of months prior to that evening, I was having a conversation with a close friend about turning 50 years old. This is a major mile-marker for many people. My friend asked me, "So, what are you planning to do for your 50th? It's only two years away. Are you going on a big trip? Are you going to have a big party? You must celebrate 50!"

I said, "I don't know. I have to think about it."

And I did think about it for a couple of weeks, searching my mind and my heart about how I wanted to celebrate half a century on Earth.

Then on Saturday evening, October 12, 2019, I sat at my dining room table on a cold and rainy night in Atlanta, with a two-finger pour of Balvenie twelve-year, single malt Scotch, and I started to write.

The words poured out of me. It was like the rusty spicket got some oil and loosened to finally turn and water flowed freely and furiously out. Not only did the words pour out, but tears.

I found myself having a good two-hour cry with each chapter. I also slept very well in the coming weeks.

I realized that I wanted to write down some things about the past 50 years so that I could make room for the next 50 years. And I also realized I wanted to do this for my son. I wanted him to know where he came from and how he came into existence, because his journey did not begin at Piedmont Hospital in Atlanta in 2008, but rather his existence began in November 1971, half-way around the world in Manila, Philippines. I also wanted him to know that his mother tried her best to leave no stone unturned. The purpose of the book finally revealed itself.

The structure of the book came easily. I knew I wanted three sections: The Women, The Men and Everyone Else.

But another thing that happened was that I did not feel compelled to tell everything. Somehow, my mind was able to view my entire life as a continuum and I just focused on selecting a moment in time on that continuum and talk about just that moment. It was razor focus and emotional. I recalled images and feelings. I recalled details of scenery, the weather, the sounds of voices and sensations, textures, and color—so much color.

This book is very revealing and personal. But not in the way that you might think. It reveals the two worlds I grew up in, the South Pacific and the Southeastern United States.

It reveals the deep sadness in my life, but also the greatest and most joyous moments. It reveals my sense of humor as well as the things I disdain.

I look forward to my next 50 years, or however long I will be around. And there may be another book in my future. I am not trying to be an author. I'm simply trying to tell a story. And furthermore, I am actually an artist. I have a degree in Theater from Agnes Scott College, but I was also a trained dancer. Communicating and telling stories through art—whether it was theater, dance or writing, are like breathing air for me. Creating is compelling for me.

I sincerely hope this book will illicit some thoughts and feelings for you, the way art is supposed to do. Thank you for giving it some of your precious time.

PART 1

The Women

CHAPTER 1

Cecelia

It was early summer of 1994. It was a perfect Saturday morning, as I recall. I was cleaning, doing laundry, and packing for my long trip back to Manila to see my father. He was very ill with lung cancer. My trip home was my college graduation gift from my mother. I had just graduated from Agnes Scott College in May and secured a new job with a public affairs firm. One of my college friends and I moved into our first apartment—a townhouse off Defoors Ferry Road, which is now quite bourgeois and renamed "West Midtown."

The call came around 9:30 a.m. It was an actual phone, mounted to the wall of the kitchen, with a long, stretched out cord and a high pitched ring.

"Hello?"

The voice responds, "Pinky, it's your Nanay."

"Hi, Mom."

"Me and Peachy are coming to Atlanta today."

"Are you coming to the farmer's market? What time?"

"No. I need to talk to you. And I need to talk to you in person."

Mom had a very thick Filipino accent. She learned

English in 1979, at the age of 41, when she immigrated with me and my sister from Manila. Mom only had a tenth-grade education, as her parents didn't believe the girls needed more than that, but ensured all the boys were educated. Ancestors are funny like that. But know this: my mom had a head for business, and she had an iron will. She played mah-jongg about twice a month. The other Filipino women would come to our small two-bedroom house on Hixson Pike Road in Chattanooga, TN. There would be Filipino food all day and *chisme* (gossip) in Tagalog. When Amy Tan published *Joy Luck Club*, I felt an instant connection to her as an author. The other author I loved was Isabel Allende, the Latina author who wrote *The House of Spirits*. Somewhere in between the pages written by these amazing women, I started to find my identity in my early twenties. Little did I know my sense of identity would be tested by God. But I don't want to jump ahead too much.

Amy and Isabel gave me a mixture of Asia and Spain, which is exactly what the Philippines is. The Philippines was conquered by the Spanish for about three centuries. There's a significant Catholic population and many words in Tagalog are Spanish words. Many names sound Hispanic. My grandmother on my mother's side was named Maria and my grandfather was named Pedro.

When we arrived in the United States in 1979, we started out in New York City. Then Mom said, "Too big. Too dangerous. Too hard. I have two girls." So, we ended up in Chattanooga, TN, where we already had some family. But growing up bi-cultural was not easy, and on this particular Saturday, it led me to ask a familiar question.

"Is everything okay? Did I do something wrong?" I asked my mother, as I had done all of my life. She was an immigrant, deeply Catholic, Filipino woman, and I had grown up completely Americanized. To make matters worse, I was educated at Girls Preparatory School, then Agnes Scott College, where the women are taught to think critically and question *everything*. Let's just say I got in trouble with my mother a lot.

"You're not in trouble. I'll see you in two hours," she said curtly and hung up.

The two hour wait for her arrival was utter torture.

She finally pulled into the driveway, but I was already at the end of the walkway, where I had been for twenty minutes, pacing.

As soon as we were inside, she said, "I brought lumpia. We eat first. You're always too skinny." Lumpia is the Filipino egg roll. It's basically heaven rolled in a thin, crispy dough and deep fried. You can add ground pork or ground beef, or make it vegetarian and just have beansprouts and cabbage. But the dough wrapping is the key.

Mom fed everyone. If you came to her house and did not eat, you were disgraceful and disrespectful. So, you starved yourself for two days before you went to her house to ensure a good appetite.

After we ate and cleaned up, she turned to my sister, "Peachy, go watch TV in the living room." Then to me, "Let's go upstairs to talk."

We climbed the stairs and sat on the edge of my bed. My comforter was hunter green and burgundy, in distinctive 1990s decorating style. I had made the matching throw pillows myself. Mom gave me her sewing machine my junior year in high school and I used to sew things, usually with straight lines only like pillows, because I didn't really know how to sew, but I wanted to sew. I had bought the fabric for my throw pillows at Forsyth Fabrics on Huff Road…oh, excuse me, "West Midtown." In 1994, my mattress and box spring were on the floor. I couldn't afford a real bedroom set yet. But I had a skinny waist and perky butt, a college degree and two jobs. So what if I didn't have real furniture?

She spits it out, "I'm not your mother."

"What?! Did Dad have an affair? I mean, *another* affair... before Gloria?"

"No. He's not your father either. You're adopted."

All the oxygen left the room. I was hot and cold at the same time, so I shivered. And then, I blinked. The identity crisis crashed all at once, and yet, everything suddenly made sense. The sensation of never feeling like I quite fit in with the rest of my family was finally explained.

"I wanted to tell you before you see your father. I was afraid he might tell you, and I wanted to be the one to tell you. I've wanted to tell you for so many years, but there was never a good time. Besides, the moment your father put you in my arms, you were mine. You have always been mine. Please don't be angry with me. I'm so sorry."

I've wanted to write about this for over twenty years, but it's hard to write through tears. Even as I write this now, I'm going through tissues. I once heard Isabel Allende speak at Agnes Scott College. She revealed how she was older when she started writing, because then it didn't make her cry as much. I never forgot that, because that's how I've felt for years.

But as I write this now, I'm not sad. I'm grateful. I had a mother, a father, and a sister. I never lacked for anything. I never felt unloved. I was too loved. I had too much. I have too much. In fact, I've always felt a bit guilty about being so blessed, and because of this I have a habit of giving. I give everything away so I'm broke, yet rich. I have a sense of urgency to serve. And that pretty much explains my entire twenty-five year career in community relations and nonprofit.

"Where did you get me?"

"From our landlady in our first apartment in Manila. We had been trying to have a baby for five years, and she knew that. Her nephew had an affair with a woman named Mila. It's short for Milagro. After you were born, they kept you a secret from their families and they didn't know what to do with you. They hired an old woman to look after you in the basement apartment. The old woman had tuberculosis, and you got it. That's when the land lady decided it was time to find you a home."

"Milagro. That means 'miracle' in Spanish."

The right side of her mouth moved upward into a smile, and she said, "I know."

I don't question the presence of God in all things, especially when my entire beginning came from "Milagro."

Mom stared far away, placing herself back in 1971 Manila, in the heat and humidity. The windows open, several humming electric fans, creating cross breezes in the one-bedroom apartment on the third floor. She had on *chinelas*. That's the Filipino word for "flip flops." My mother's *chinelas* were semi-automatic weapons that met my skinny behind like lightening until I was a freshman in high school. It only stopped then because I finally had enough leg strength to outrun her.

She continued, "Your father came home from work one day. She stopped him in the driveway and just asked him if we wanted a baby. Your father went with her to the basement apartment. He took you, a few blankets, and these things."

Mom went into her purse, pulled out an envelope, and dumped the contents on the bed.

I immediately saw a plastic band, the kind they put on the ankles of newborn babies to label them. It was pink.

It said, "Baby Girl. Cecelia Milagro. November 6, _____"
That was my real name. But was it who I was? Who the hell was I?

"November?! But my birthday is December 6! I'm a Sagittarius not a Scorpio!" The identity crisis raged.

Mom explained that's when they got my birth certificate and then she renamed me Maria Lourdes. She named me after Saint Lourdes, one of her favorite saints. And of course, Maria, because almost all Filipino Catholic girls are named Maria first, then a patron saint name and last name of the father. My sister was Maria Theresa, God rest her soul. This naming configuration confused Americans like hell. And when my sister and I were getting registered for school in America, the registrar always had a million questions about why we were both named "Maria," which I had to answer for my mother at age eight. I learned English in six months, and she was still learning. Young immigrants often carry the burden of the family. They are the first ones to learn the language and the rules of engagement. Then they have to help the rest of the family along, while at the same time balancing respect and honor to the elders. It was like that for me at eight years old. I grew up in two worlds.

As I sat on the bed realizing that I was not who I thought I was, I didn't cry. I couldn't cry. Mom told me later that it worried her. She also told me she would never forget the look on my face, looking through the screen door of my apartment, as she left later that day. But I did cry on the next day and for two days straight.

Things happened very fast after that. I convinced my mother to go back with me and show me the apartment in Manila. I begged her to track down any family I might have. We found a distant cousin. Her name was Pilar. But I remember the feeling when I met her. I saw features of my face on her face. Our complexions were the same. We shared the high forehead, narrow shoulders and petite build. We were the same. A total stranger who was the same.

After meeting her, I wanted to meet others. I begged my mother to help me find others. Then she said, "No."

"Why?!" I exclaimed.

"Because you are a secret. If you find them, you will be invading their lives. You could hurt them. Why would you want to hurt others? Especially when you have a family. Are we not enough for you anymore?"

I paused. I stammered, "But...I want to know."

She said, "I won't help you find any others. But if you want to do it, I won't stop you."

In 1994, Ancestry or 23andMe did not exist. I didn't know how I would go about searching for more relatives. Today, this technology is available at my fingertips, but I won't do it. The only reason I would ever do it is to save my son's life for health reasons. But even then, there is family on his father's side we could go to first. But I applaud people who go on a search for relatives. That takes courage and I understand the need for a sense of belonging and satisfying curiosity. I understand that impulse deeply. I also understand there may be other reasons why people go on a search, but no matter what the reason, there's no "right" reason or "wrong" reason. Just a reason.

I remember I didn't sleep a wink that night after my mother said that. I kept churning on the sentence, "You're a secret."

A secret...a secret...a secret that could hurt others. I told myself in the dark, "Maria, you can't hurt others. You can't go back. You can't go backwards. You have to go forwards. You have to go back to America and go forward."

How many thousands of immigrants have this same thought every night, as they lie wide awake, but don't have *this* mother?

A week later, my mom and my sister left the Philippines and went back to Chattanooga. I stayed another week with my father before flying home.

It was the longest trip of my life. It was twenty four hours of travel, with layovers in Korea and Alaska. I was by myself and spent the entire trip in my thoughts. I talked to myself in the dim light of the plane cabin, allowing the baritone whooshing sound of the 747 to lull my thoughts, "You're going forward. No more looking back. You can't go backwards."

I never went back to the Philippines after that.

I came back to Atlanta and worked my public affairs job during the day and a retail job at night. Being fresh out of college with an arts degree meant having two jobs.

Atlanta was buzzing with so much excitement and growth. And it wasn't just Atlanta, it was the entire region. The Olympic Games were coming in less than two years. The leaders of the region didn't just spur economic development. They united a region. We were welcoming the whole world to our city, and we wanted to put our best foot forward. This was the climate when I returned from my trip to Manila.

Looking back on that time, I now realize that what was an identity crisis for a few weeks of my life was not a crisis at all. It was just God at the wheel. I could not have appreciated the 1990s in Atlanta if He hadn't made it personal for me. I would not have seen the true beauty of the changing landscape of my environment if He didn't reveal for me the rest of the picture and then give me room on the canvas to create the rest of the picture.

And He also gave me this mother. For all her Catholic and Filipino conservative hang ups, she was actually incredibly progressive and forward thinking. She said it was because she didn't want my father to tell me about my adoption, but I think she knew I was about to start my life, and she felt I should finally know the truth.

By early fall, when Atlanta didn't have extended summer days, the colors and the air changed. Everything seemed crisper, like a camera lens rotating left and right until the image was in perfect focus. The picture was the city mobilizing and moving forward, and I planned to go with it.

 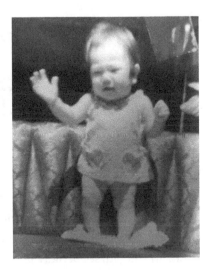

Photos of me the day after adoption. Manila, 1971.

CHAPTER 2

Cila

There was a small town in the Philippines called Bulacan. The car rides from Manila to Bulacan felt like eternity to me as a small child when my family and I would go there to visit my mother's side of the family. My mother would carry extra *suhol* in her purse, which is the Tagalog word for "bribe." The bribe money was for the traffic cops who would stop people traveling from Manila back into the villages. They knew people from Manila had money. We were fortunate. Our family had money. We had a driver and an air conditioned car, which was a huge luxury in the South Pacific Islands. So when our family traveled from the city into the village, we were targets for overworked and underpaid cops who oversaw law and order under the regime of Ferdinand Marcos, the famous dictator. He was probably not as famous as his wife, Imelda Marcos, who was found with over 2,000 pairs of shoes. Imelda might be a distant cousin to me, judging by the contents of my closet, the number of shoes and handbags. But I digress...

My memory of Bulacan is exactly what one would expect a village in the Philippines to look like in the 1970s. Sunkissed, brown children playing in the road. Motor tricycles shuttling people to and from the marketplace. Little house *tiendas*. These were small five and dime businesses that sold sundries like toothpaste, cigarettes, gum, and my favorite, frozen ice treats, which were basically Kool-aid poured into long strips of plastic and then put in the freezer. They were five cents each, and Mom always gave me ten cents. I would run to the house two doors down from my grandparents' house and buy an ice treat from the *tienda*, go find an open window sill where I could sit and hang my legs out, tear open one end of the plastic, and savor the frozen ice treat. The banana leaves swayed back and forth in the breeze while I ignored the small trickles of sweat down my back. The chickens in the back cluck-cluck-clucked.

It was in this village that Priscila was born on January 17, 1937. They called her "Cila" (Cee-Lah). This was just two years before WWII and just a few years before Japan invaded the Philippines. The Japanese were harsh, to say the least. My mother once alluded to a bad memory involving a Japanese soldier and her aunt. I never pressed her much for details I didn't need to know. Some bad memories should be left alone. All Filipinos thank God for General Douglas MacArthur, who came to save the brown people of the Philippines from Japanese occupation in 1944. There is a famous memorial statue of General MacArthur at Leyte Memorial Park, commemorating his landing on the islands. The statues are all very tall Americans in army uniforms, rising out of the Pacific Ocean, coming to save my people.

My grandmother had 13 children in total, but only 9 survived. There were 6 boys and 3 girls. My mother was the second to the oldest of the girls. My oldest aunt was Rosita, who never married and was a virgin her entire life. Her entire life! And my youngest aunt was Erlinda who married and had three boys herself.

My grandmother birthed all the children in the house with a midwife and no drugs. Let that sink in for a moment.

In the early 1950s when Cila was about 14, she met Luis. They locked eyes at church. He started courting her and they fell in love. My aunt Rosita did not like Luis and she was quite vocal about it. My mother told me, "She thought he was ugly."

He might have been ugly, but he got his engineering degree, moved to California, and had good fortune. However, I wouldn't be here if my mother ended up with Luis. But then again, my mother might have been happier if she had followed her heart.

My aunt Rosita succeeded in breaking up the young romantics by causing a fight between the two of them. My mother never forgot that fight. A very light pool of mist would gather in the inner corner of her eyes when she would recall that memory.

She said, "We were screaming by the river. I got so mad. I threw the ring he gave me into the river. I told him I would never speak to him again, which I didn't for thirty years. I decided I would go into the convent and marry God."

She did just that. When I say my mother is a deeply Catholic Filipino woman, I don't mean that she is 100 percent. It's more like 120 percent. I have always believed mom truly communed with God. She would light candles and pray, and all her prayers were always answered. Always. It felt great to have a mother who was favored by God. Some of that favor transferred to me.

Cila was beautiful. Her family were light skinned Filipinos with round shaped eyes, not almond shaped eyes like most Asians. It was believed there was a lot of Spanish blood in the family, which made sense given the very Spanish last name.

She entered the convent and was sequestered along with the other novices. Not even her family could see her. Family and friends could drop off letters and food with the Mother

Superior, who checked all the items to ensure God would approve, and then give them to the novices.

It was through the Mother Superior that Luis decided to reach my mother. He knew he couldn't do it through her family, not with my aunt Rosita, the guard dog.

On a normal, hot, and humid day in 1950s Philippines, Luis collected fresh eggs from the chicken coop, something every Filipino family had. He picked a brown egg, carefully drilled a tiny hole on both ends, then drained the egg white and egg yoke from the eggshell, allowing it to dry completely. The yoke came out of the eggshell slower than condensed milk out of a can. This took days.

Then he took a small piece of paper, and with his practiced and meticulous engineering handwriting, composed a love letter in as many lines as could fit on that small piece of paper. He rolled up the paper until it was the size of a match stick and threaded it carefully into the eggshell.

He got a basket for all the eggs and nestled them into some cloth in the basket to prevent them from breaking. He put on his Barong Tagalog, which is a traditional, light cotton, embroidered shirt, worn for formal occasions by Filipino men, his good pants, and his good shoes. He put pomade in his hair, combing a perfectly straight part on the left side of his head.

There was a special side door to the convent where family and friends dropped off the goods for the novices. It had three stone steps leading up to a big wooden door with an iron cross. The Mother Superior herself would take the baskets and speak to the messengers.

"Mother, I am Luis. I am Cila's cousin. I brought her eggs," extending his arms, carefully holding the basket with both hands.

"God bless you, Luis. We will give Cila your gift." She took the basket solemnly from his hands, never cracking an egg, or a smile. Then she turned to another nun and handed her the basket. The novices were seated inside the rectory, where they could see this entire ritual.

My mother told me, "When I saw him, my throat tightened up and my stomach flipped. I didn't know what he was doing there, and I was so afraid the nuns would find out. And then I would be so ashamed in the eyes of God."

But the nuns didn't find out. Cila got her basket of eggs.

"I looked in the basket and there were 6 eggs. 4 white, 1 light blue, and 1 brown egg. I will never forget it. I picked up each egg, looking for something underneath because I knew it couldn't be just a basket of eggs. And when I picked up the brown egg, it was lighter than the others. I broke the shell and inside was his message."

I was a teenager in America when mom told me this story. I remember sitting on the green scratchy couch in our small house in Chattanooga, and the Solid Gold dancers were just coming on the television. I normally dropped whatever I was doing when the dancers came on. I wanted to be a Solid Gold dancer from the time I was ten years old, and I would prance around in my room, in my ballet leotard repeating the dance moves, or what I thought were dance moves. But that night, I was riveted by her story, and I got up from the couch to turn down the volume. The television was a 1980s color set with a wood encasing and no remote control. It weighed a ton. When it stopped working, my mother covered it with one of her crocheted table cloths and put the new television on top of it, and kept on rolling.

"What did the letter say?!" I sat back down on the couch on the end by the lamp and tucked my legs under me.

"It said, 'Marry me. Don't marry God. I love you.'"

How direct and romantic at the same time on that small piece of paper.

"Is that why you never became a nun?"

"No. I got very ill and the nuns sent me back to my family."

"If you didn't become a nun, then why didn't you marry Luis?"

Mom cocked her head to the left a little bit as if she was examining an expensive piece of art, sighed deeply, and then became the strong woman again and said, "Enough questions. Luis is in the past. That's all in the past. I married your father and had my girls. That's all that matters and that's all you need to know."

The wonky sound of a needle sliding off the record played in my head. She abruptly stopped the musicality of this story, and I was left feeling unfulfilled. Later on, as I played this story over and over in my mind, I came to realize this was an unresolved story of love. It would have been unfair for me to pressure my mother for more details.

Luis did try to reach out to my mother on several occasions, including a ten-page letter thirty years later, which he managed to send to her through a mutual friend. He married someone else and had three children. Rumor was he never got over my mother, and when he had too many drinks, he would cry out her name.

There are a million stories I could tell you about Cila, believe me. But I choose this one. And I chose this one several years ago. Why? Because I believe in love stories. Every single woman deserves a good love story. Every single woman should have a Luis in her past, present or future. As women, we are built for love. We are built to shoulder heartbreak. Our love for the men in our lives is part of what completes us. I'm not saying it's everything, I'm just saying love stories are part of the journey. It took me years to see my mother as a woman and not just my mother. It took me years to see her in my mind's eye as young, giggly, flirty, in love, and passionate.

Luis gave my mother true, passionate love. Later she would meet my father and fall in love again. Both men brought her joy and sadness, but they completed her story.

Cila, circa 1967, Manila.

CHAPTER 3

Theresa

My parents built our house in Manila in an area called Quezon City in a nice, upper middle-class neighborhood, with indoor plumbing. This included a rain reservoir tank just for our house. The streets were lined with palm trees, and mom had gardens in the front and back, both connected by a koi pond that ran under the house. The pond had lily pads and frogs. The back garden had a babbling brook fountain and a statue of the Virgin Mary. The house was two levels with four bedrooms. There was the master suite, a children's room, a mother in-law room, and a room for the cook and my nanny. It had two kitchens, an indoor kitchen and dining room, and an outdoor kitchen and eating area in the back. The men who worked on the property stayed in another smaller house across the street. The house had a stone wall surrounding it, and a huge two car garage. And in the garage, hung a stone sculpture with our family initials. For the Philippines, it was quite luxurious.

My mother had a head for business. She always wanted to have her own money and not depend on my father, so she opened her own *tienda*. The *tienda* was to the side of the big

car garage. My dad had two cars and a big truck. One of the
cars was a 1967 red Mustang. For the record, I was never quite
sure what my father did for a living, but it had something to
do with upcycling scrap metal and other recyclable things like
electronics, etc. I'm sure there was other "business," as well.

My mother's tienda sold rice, cigarettes, candy, gum, and
other sundries, but my favorite were the little ice cream cups
with the little wooden spoons. One time, my mother laid down
for her afternoon nap, and I used a chair to climb up to the
freezer, where I knew the ice cream was kept. I ate all the ice
cream. When she woke up, I got in a lot of trouble and paid
for my sins through the slap-slap-slap of the *chinela* from her
right foot.

One of my fondest memories about the *tienda* was going
with her to buy the rice. Two of the men who worked for our
household would drive us in the big truck and we would go
to the mill. Bump, bump, bump in the truck we would be for
about an hour until we got to the factory. The factory was loud
and dusty.

There, my mother would look at the giant sacks of jade rice.
She carried a sifter, and she would sift through the jade rice
looking for mites and worms before she purchased the sack.
After she picked out her good sacks of rice, the men would
load the sacks on the truck and take us back to the *tienda*. She
sold the rice by the pound to people in the neighborhood. Her
tienda was very lucrative.

On the other side of the house, mom had a hair salon.
She had two dryers and a wash sink. And the entire salon was
pink, as if a bottle of Pepto Bismol threw up in there. Mom
got her beautician license in her late twenties and also went to
secretary school. She could perm and type 100 words/minute.
Still, no high school diploma. This would not become an issue
until we moved to America.

As the only child of the *Amo* and *Ama*, which are Tagalog for heads of household for the man and woman, I was somewhat the little princess. I ran through that house like a whirling dervish. My nanny chased after me, making sure I didn't break anything and that nothing broke me. No one was allowed to spank me, except for my mother. No one. My mother ran the house, and that included all the women and children who worked in the house. My father wasn't even allowed to spank me or give orders to the women who worked in the house. Everything went through the *Ama*.

One time, mom went to mass when I was taking a nap. When I woke up, she was gone and I had a meltdown. My nanny couldn't console me. No one could console me. Finally, my father lost his temper and used his belt. I had welts across the tops of my thighs. When my mother got home from mass and she saw my legs, she whipped around and smacked my father in the face. He never spanked me again, but then again, I never pushed my father that hard again. I didn't want to get *him* in trouble.

When I was almost five years old, my mother called me into her room. She had me sit on the bed, which was covered in a chartreuse green, polyester, slippery comforter. It matched the drapes and carpet, and the bed was a white wood frame with gold trim.

"Pinky, come here." She put me in her lap.

"I have good news. You're going to have a baby brother. We're going to call him, 'Junior.'"

"Can I play with him?"

"Yes. But you have to be gentle at first, because he will be very small."

I thought to myself, "Oh, goodie, a new playmate."

Soon after that, the house was a buzz with excitement of a new baby coming into the family. The nanny and cook were constantly cleaning the floors and wiping every speck of dust. They washed all the linens every week in big soapy tubs in the back outdoor kitchen and hung them to dry on the lines. There were deliveries all the time, including a white wooden crib, lots of cloth diapers, and pins. I remember being told explicitly to never play with the diaper pins.

It wasn't a boy. It was a girl. Mom and Dad wanted a boy, and they prayed for a boy, but God had other plans. My sister came into the world on October fifth, which happens to also be my Aunt Rosita's birthday. Everyone in the family saw this as a good omen because Aunt Rosita was rich.

When they brought her home, I thought, "How can there be so much noise coming out of that little thing? And how am I supposed to play with that?"

But she was a beautiful baby. She had the same round shaped eyes of my mother's side and the dark thick hair from my father's side. Her baby skin so supple, and her feet were so cute. I loved her feet. I bit her on the foot when she was a baby and got in trouble, and got a slap, slap, slap with the *chinela*.

Mom said, "She will be Maria Theresa, my other favorite saint. But we will call her 'Peachy' so we have a 'Pinky' and 'Peachy.'"

And so, my sister and I were Pinky and Peachy. I kept the name Pinky until I graduated from Agnes Scott College. I got this nickname because I was very rosy and pink when I was a baby. I was also a very fat baby, like a little Buddha. I basically spent the next thirty years growing into all the fat and rolled up skin God gave me from the beginning. I changed my name to Maria, mainly because I didn't think I could get a job with a name like "Pinky" without anyone thinking I was a stripper. So when I get those Facebook memes about "What would your stripper name be?" Well, guess what? I have one. Given to me by my mother, thank you very much.

One afternoon, my mother was working in her *tienda*, and I was in the garage playing with a baby chick. The nanny was keeping an eye on my sister, who was taking a nap. Oh man, the baby chicks were so cute! You could buy them at *palenque*, which is the Tagalog word for fresh market. My mother loved to go to the *palenque* and buy fresh fish, vegetables, fruits, and baby chicks for me to play with. She would put empty soda boxes under the gate so they wouldn't escape the garage while I chased them around. When I caught them, I would hug them tightly and kiss them to death. Sometimes I literally played with them until their death. The little chicks who survived me playing with them went on to the chicken coop, where they grew up to be contributing members of the coop. This activity kept me occupied for *hours*. In retrospect, I realize this must seem inhumane to allow a five-year old to play with baby chicks until they died. But this is my childhood in Manila, and I can't change the past.

A messenger walked up to the window of the *tienda* and asked for my mother. He was delivering a letter. It was from a woman named Gloria. Her letter confessed a love affair with my father. My mother fell apart at the seams. She wailed in the *tienda*, then ran upstairs to the master bedroom, where she wailed the rest of the afternoon until my father came home. Then the fighting started. The next year would be some of the most difficult memories I had as a child. My mother was inconsolable. She tried to leave my father and go to other parts of the islands, but he would always find her and convince her to come back. One day he said to her, "Just give up trying to leave me, and forgive me already. You know you can't survive on your own. You have everything here."

He was quite wrong. So very, very wrong.

When I was seven and my sister was two, my dad came home from work one afternoon in 1979. My mother, my sister, and I were sitting in the living room. My sister and I had on matching t-shirts with our names "Pinky" and "Peachy" airbrushed on the back in cursive. We also had on matching bell bottom denim pants. Also in the living room were two forty-pound boxes, carefully taped and tied with cord, and two very large hard blue Samsonite suitcases.

My father asked, "What is this?"

My mother answered flatly, "I'm leaving you."

"Where do you think you're going?"

"To America. The Philippines is not big enough, and you keep finding me. I'm going to get away from you. You committed adultery, and I will not be with a sinner. I have the visas, passports, and $2000.00. My relatives in New York are waiting for us. You can take us to the airport and say goodbye to the children, or you can say goodbye to them now, and I can call a cab."

I remember my father crying. I was crying. My sister was crying. My mother didn't shed one tear. This is the reason I love the Mary Chapin Carpenter song, "He Thinks He'll Keep Her." The song is about a woman who played a good housewife until it was time for change. I sing along to that song often.

The migration from Manila to New York City was incredible. It took twenty-four hours. My body wasn't used to the cool, dry air of the plane, and the April temperatures of the Americas was freezing cold to me. My little brown body craved the 100-degree temperature and the moist humidity of the Islands. My lips chapped badly.

The American stewardess (which is what they were called then, not "flight attendants") on our flight from California to New York said to me, "Honey, you need Chapstick." What the hell was Chapstick?

Once in New York, we didn't stay long. After a few weeks,

Mom decided it was too big a place for us. By May 1979, we were in Chattanooga, Tennessee.

We had lots of family there, and we were always at family gatherings. We lived with my cousin Susan for a while who was a nurse at Erlanger Hospital. Many of my family (many Filipinos) are in the healthcare field. My extended family flocked to Chattanooga because of the Erlanger Health System.

When my sister was three or four years old, we were at my cousin Jenny and Oscar's house. Jenny was a medical technician, and Oscar had a European car dealership with some of his brothers. Rice was cooking in the pressure cooker, and adobo chicken was in the pot. The adults were all in the dining room playing mah-jongg, and the kids were playing in the den. We were roughhousing when suddenly, my sister hit her head hard on a corner of a stand-up organ. My mother and cousins did their best to console her and got her down for a nap. Little did we know she had a concussion. Going to sleep with a concussion is very bad. In the middle of night, she started having seizures.

The ambulance came to Mansion Hills Apartments, where we were staying with my cousin. The paramedics rushed to the bedroom and checked her vitals. I was terrified and hid in the big closet, in between the hanging clothes, clinging to the reddish orange shag carpet of the apartment.

From that point on, my sister was disabled. She had suffered an irreversible brain injury. My mother and I, mostly my mother, would spend the next 28 years caring for her. In retrospect, it was God's will that my mother have a purpose in life, because I didn't need my mother as much. I was decidedly independent, and my mother needed to be needed.

Peachy was ambulatory, could learn skills, and was able to write and read a little. In the 1980s, she was referred to as "retarded." Even back then when it was widely accepted to say such things, it hurt my feelings.

Peachy gave the best hugs. When she hugged you, she did it with all her being. She also loved to laugh, and though she was disabled, she still had common sense. She used to be my conscience. She would always give me this look when she knew I was doing something I wasn't supposed to be doing behind my mother's back. She would point at me with her right pointer finger and say, "No. No. No."

I would usually reply in a hushed and insistent voice, "Shhh. Don't tell mom."

Peachy never told on me. She was a loyal and sweet sister, but she also did not want to get in the middle of things between my mother and me. She knew God gave my mother eyes in the back of her head, and that my mischievous self would be no match to the slap-slap-slap of the *chinela*.

Peachy loved my ex-husband, Tony. She liked it when I would bring him home to visit, especially at Christmas. I look back on why she enjoyed it so much, and I think it was because it made the household an even number. My sister didn't feel like the third wheel as much, and she had someone who would sit with her while my mother and I chattered in Tagalog about things, usually arguing or gossiping.

Tony endured many Filipino Christmases. One Christmas, Peachy went up to him in the middle of Christmas dinner and asked him to follow her to her room. She said she needed his help. So Tony and I both followed her to the bedroom. She pointed at the big dresser, and said, "Move that, please."

Tony asked, "Move it? Move it to where?"

Peachy responded, "From the wall."

Tony moved the dresser away from the wall, and there behind it were several pencils, a notebook, and other things which had rolled off the dresser and fallen behind it. She couldn't reach them, and she waited for the next opportunity to see him to ask him to do her this favor. Common sense.

In school, Peachy was placed in special education classes. She graduated with a high school degree. Her graduation was a huge accomplishment, and I remember I wore my "Nancy Reagan red suit" I bought from Petite Sophisticate when Casual Corner still had a petite store.

In the first week of December, 2007, my mother called me, "Pinky, I need you and Tony to come home. Peachy is getting a routine hysterectomy. She will never have babies and she doesn't need to keep worrying about her periods. Also, her doctor is recommending this because her periods are very heavy. It will be in a week."

"Okay, Mom. No problem. We'll be there."

Tony and I took mom to lunch at Olive Garden by Hamilton Place Mall while Peachy was in surgery. We were seated in a booth. We were anxiously waiting out the time until we could go back to the hospital and meet her in recovery. Then my cell phone rang.

"Hello?"

"Is this Maria?"

"Yes."

"This is Dr._____. I'm the surgeon for your sister, Theresa. I'm calling you from the operating room. We have found cancerous tumors inside your sister which have spread throughout her stomach and parts of her lungs. We need your permission to perform further surgery so we can remove as much of it as possible."

My stomach dropped through the floor of the leather seats of the booth. I looked at my mother.

She asked, "What is it?"

I remained calm and said, "Nothing, Mom. They just need a little bit more time in surgery." I was still the eight-year old immigrant girl who learned to speak English first, taking care of her family. And at that moment, I had to be more in charge than ever.

The doctor concluded, "We should be done in about four hours."

"Okay, doctor. We'll be there."

I hung up. Tony and I glanced at each other. He knew something was wrong. By then, he and I had learned to communicate just by looking at each other. I finally turned to my mother, who was not fooled by my composure either.

"Mom, they found something inside Peachy."

"What?!"

"They found some cancerous tumors, and they are going to remove them. It should be fine. We are lucky they found them now and can perform the surgery. It will take a few more hours, but we can wait here."

"No! We have to go to the hospital now!" She started to slide out of the booth, clutching her purse.

"Mom, we have to pay the bill. Wait! Tony, get the bill. Mom, slow down."

She ran out of the restaurant and stopped at the car when she realized the doors were locked and I had the keys. We rushed back to the hospital, hurrying up to wait.

We went to the main reception first to identify ourselves and asked for the recovery room. The main desk had Christmas garland. Candy canes hung on the edge of the counter below a mechanical, distracting Santa Claus on the desk. I had never felt disdain for the Christmas holidays as much as I did at that moment. And I am still presently trying to create new Christmas holiday memories so I can soothe that memory.

We found the recovery room, and we waited for her there. Mom paced the room back and forth, back and forth, back and forth.

When they wheeled Peachy's big hospital bed into the room, she had several tubes and IV's.

The nurses were cheerful, the lead surgeon not as much. He had the oncologist with him.

I would say the two doctors could have benefitted from some sensitivity training, but frankly, is there any good way to deliver bad news? I feel for health care professionals who have to deliver bad news all the time. How do you tell someone their loved one is dying? And how must these health workers feel on their end, having to deliver this kind of news often?

"Ms. Balais..." He was looking at me, not my mother, but my mother was hovering and listening intently.

"I'm sorry to inform you, but we have determined the cancer is pretty advanced. We need to do an oncology report to determine the root of the problem, but it has spread to her stomach and lungs. You can choose to do palliative care or cancer treatment as soon as possible."

"What do you mean? Do you mean hospice or chemo?"

"Yes, ma'am."

My mom exclaimed, "What is chemo?!"

"It's cancer medicine, Mom."

"Then, yes! Yes! Yes! We need the cancer medicine. Whatever to save my baby!"

Peachy was her baby. She was the only surviving biological child between my mother and father. There was also my baby sister, Gemma. But Gemma was born prematurely and didn't survive. Gemma is buried in a family cemetery in Manila.

Unlike me, my mother carried Peachy in her belly. She nursed her, raised her, and cared for her full-time after the brain injury. Peachy was my mother's true purpose in life.

I turned to the doctor and asked, "Doctor, what are the chances?"

"Honestly, we would need to see the oncology report to

make a full determination." I looked at the oncologist, who had not said a single word but was saying volumes. I realized they had *already made a determination.*

My mother desperately pleaded, "Yes! Do it! We want the chemo. We have to fight."

I turned to the doctor without saying a word. We locked eyes. I understood that he was saying there was really no chance. I communicated silently that I understood, but we had to do this for my mother. I dropped my chin, staring, and cocked my head a little to the left. This was my "It will be so" look. And it was so. We started chemo the next week.

I found out I was pregnant in early February, 2008. By that time, I was driving to Chattanooga every single weekend to see my mother and sister, and I called every single day.

On a cool February Saturday, I was home visiting. Home Health Care had installed a home hospital bed for Peachy in my mother's bedroom. When I came to visit, I slept in the other room, in my sister's usual bed, which was a lovely oak single bed frame that now belongs to my son.

I snuggled up to my sister in her home hospital bed, and I whispered in her ear, "I have a secret to tell you."

She cracked a smile. Peachy's smiles were the best.

"I'm pregnant."

Her smile got bigger. And she tried to sit up from the bed, but I laid my arm across her chest and hugged her.

Later that day, I told my mother I was pregnant. She was lukewarm. My feelings weren't hurt by her lukewarm reaction. I knew she was under a lot of stress, but I had hoped the news that she would become a grandmother could bring her some light.

She hugged me. She put on a light jacket and left the house for a walk in the misty February afternoon.

When she came back twenty minutes later, her hair was

moist and clung to her head. She said to me, "Peachy is going to die. God already has a soul to take her place. This is what we believed in my village." My mother was making peace with the idea she would bury her own child in a few months.

My sister was in and out of the hospital for several months, and we had home care. It was a very stressful time.

On May 4, 2008, Tony and I were having dinner with some friends at a pizza place in downtown Atlanta in a historic area called the Fairlie-Poplar District. The main streets were Fairlie Street and Poplar Street, behind the Federal Court Building. The streets were old brick. There were several historic buildings within a two block radius, including the Fairlie-Poplar Building which was converted to very nice residential lofts. The pizza place was called "Sliced Pizza," and it was about five blocks from our loft on Marietta Street. After the Olympics, there was a resurgence of intown living. Many people moved back into the city and bought into the city-loft-living lifestyle. Tony and I were some of the first ones to do this. We moved into the Metropolitan on Marietta Street, another historic building redeveloped into residential space to house workers for the Olympics. Buildings like this were placed on the market after the Olympics for leased lofts, and then eventually for owned condos. The historic Jacob's Pharmacy where the first Coca-Cola ever sold was adjacent to our loft building. We were considered "Urban Pioneers." Some of our dearest and closest friends came out of that time in our lives. Our neighbors united around The Atlanta Downtown Neighborhood Association. We planned neighborhood arts festivals, did park clean-ups, and enjoyed several glasses of wine and many martinis. We were with these wonderful friends at a sidewalk table one beautiful evening in May when my cell phone rang.

"Hello, this is Maria."

"Ms. Balais?"

"Yes."

"I'm nurse____, from Erlanger Hospital in Chattanooga. I'm calling about your sister, Theresa."

"Yes, is everything okay?"

"Well, no ma'am. Your sister is in critical condition and she is in ICU. And your mother...well, your mother really needs some support."

"I understand, but I'm in Atlanta. It's 9:00p.m., and I'm pregnant and don't feel comfortable driving to Chattanooga tonight. Can I come as soon as possible tomorrow?"

"Yes ma'am, whatever you feel you need to do. But I recommend you call other family to be with your mother if you can."

"Yes, I will. Also, nurse? Max out the morphine, Demerol, Percocet, whatever cocktail you need to pump into my sister so she is not in pain."

"Yes, ma'am. We will do everything we can to keep your sister comfortable."

"Okay, thank you so much. I'll make some calls. I'll be there tomorrow."

I hung up and immediately called my cousin, Susan. She was at work, but one of her daughters was able to go to the hospital.

I rushed to the loft to send an email to my work and inform them about my family emergency. I was at Troutman Sanders at this time, and my boss was very understanding. She was aware my sister had been very ill.

I packed a suitcase, including whatever dressy maternity clothes I had, including a funeral outfit. The drive up to Chattanooga was a blur. I wasn't worried about my sister. God had the wheel, as always. I was thinking about my mother.

I went straight to the hospital. Erlanger Memorial Hospital

was founded in 1881 through the generosity of a French Nobleman, Baron Frederic Emile d'Erlanger. The nobleman had several financial interests in railroad companies in the Southeast region, and he donated $5,000 to help build a new hospital. In today's dollars, that would be $4 million. The hospital was named after his Southern wife, the Baroness Erlanger. I saw her portrait and read the history of this hospital many times, while wandering the atrium halls of the hospital on the many visits for my sister, and then later my mother. I grew fond of the Baroness's portrait and silently thanked her for having laid the cornerstone of that hospital. It had literally become a second home for my family.

At the entry of the ICU level of the hospital, the light changed. In the center of the floor was a pod where all the nurses, doctors, and other healthcare professionals worked. It had several computer monitors and charts. That area was brightly lit. Against the walls were the ICU hospital beds, separated by walls, but all glass in the front so the hospital staff could see directly into the rooms. That area was dimly lit.

I walked up to the nurses' station with my driver's license in my hand. I knew the drill. They confirmed my Power of Attorney and showed me to my sister's room.

My mother was seated in a chair in the room, her rosary draped in her right hand.

I looked at her eyes to see how much she might have been crying. But oddly enough, they just looked tired and not red or swollen as I expected.

I crossed the room and kissed her on the cheek.

I whispered to her, "Nanay."

She replied in a hoarse voice, "Pinky."

I walked over to my sister. Her bed was in a 20 degree angle, so she wasn't lying flat. She was on life support. Her lungs had given out, and she was being sustained by a machine.

Her fingers were very blue. Oxygen was no longer getting to her extremities.

I turned to my mother and said in a soothing voice, "Mom, we can't keep doing this. We have to let her go."

Mom got up from the chair and walked over to me, then reached down and placed her hand on my pregnant belly. I was wearing a long sleeve, coral maternity blouse with a sash. It was from Ann Taylor, and it was my favorite maternity blouse.

Mom rested her hand on my belly for a minute, and then she took a long breath and said, "I know." Then she removed her hand from my belly and turned and walked out of the room to the end of the hall. She sat down by the window in the family waiting area. She stared out the window and watched the rain clouds roll in.

I went to the nurses' station and asked for the attending physician. Because of HIPPA laws we spoke privately inside my sister's room.

"Doctor, we will take her off life support."

"Okay. You will need to sign some paperwork."

"Okay."

"And you will need to sit in the waiting area as we remove her from the support. When we are done, we will call you back in, and you can sit with her until the end."

"Okay."

I joined my mother in the waiting room. The room had rows of connected faux leather seats and side tables. There were no soda machines or snack vending machines. There was no food and drink allowed in the ICU area. We sat in silence. The rosary was draped in her right hand.

Twenty minutes later, a nurse came to get us from the waiting room and escorted us back to the hospital room.

All the tubes were gone, except for a machine that beeped. Peachy lay in the bed with the hospital blankets folded neatly under her arms. Her arms were limp, fingers blue. Mom and I placed our purses in the chair and walked to the hospital bed. My mother went to Peachy's left side, and I went to her right. Mom took her left hand, with her left hand, and then she placed her rosary in my sister's hand. I took Peachy's left hand with both my hands. Mom and I didn't speak.

89beep...beep...80...beep...beep...beep...75...beep...beep...beep...70...beep...beeeeep....beeeeeeeeeeeeeeee.....echoes....and then....stillness. And I felt her soul float up and out.

When it was over, the nurses came into the room. They had a monitor at the station and knew she had passed. I recall signing more paperwork, including naming the funeral home we had chosen.

I drove my mother home. We silently changed into our pajamas. We made hot chocolate and ate pandesal. I said to Mom, "I will handle the funeral arrangements."

She said, "Yes, I know. Thank God for you."

Then we went to bed. My mother slept hard for eight hours straight. She had not slept for five months.

The week of the funeral was very fast paced. It was a beautiful funeral. Peachy had a white casket with lavender and yellow roses. Our longtime clergyman Father Rudisil had retired, so Father Schmidt held the mass.

During the process of the funeral, I was aware that it was more for my mother and not my sister. And really, that's what funerals are. They are for the living, not the dead. When things calmed down later on, I noticed Mom didn't go to mass or light any candles at home. She was mad at God. She also began to let go of her mind. She hung on for another three years or so, just enough to meet my son and allow him to form some memories of his grandmother, who he calls *Lola*, which is Tagalog for grandmother.

I wear black all the time, and people say, "Oh, Maria with her chic black dresses and outfits." Yes, black is chic and simple, and I often say that Audrey Hepburn is my style icon. There is a lot of truth to that. But the truth is that I've been in mourning for years.

My sweet sister, Maria Theresa (Peachy)

CHAPTER 4

Virginia

Virginia was born on April 13, 1906 in Roswell, Georgia. Her family lived in an antebellum mansion in Roswell called Bulloch Hall. Today, Bulloch Hall is maintained by the Roswell Historical Society. It is exactly what you might imagine a southern, antebellum mansion would look like with a lush, rolling, green lawn, big porches with tall columns, big windows for hot summer days, and beautiful working fireplaces for cooler months. It had elegant staircases at the front of the house for the family, and a staircase in the back of the house for servants. The wood floors creaked with age. Mittie Bulloch married U.S. President Theodore Roosevelt in that mansion and stood on the fifth wood plank from the tiled edge of the fireplace.

Virginia attended a women's college called Agnes Scott College in the 1920s. While at Agnes Scott, she met her future husband George Power. George went to the Georgia Institute of Technology, a "Ramblin' Wreck from Georgia Tech," but left Atlanta for a short while to get his business degree from The Wharton School of Business in Philadelphia. He came back to Atlanta to marry Virginia in the late 1920s. Eventually, they moved to Chattanooga, Tennessee. They never had children.

George opened an advertising agency and purchased an old brownstone building on a hill overlooking the Tennessee River. It was situated in Bluff View, the art district in Chattanooga.

George and Virginia were part of the Greatest Generation. They endured the Great Depression and were frugal and modest, characteristics of truly wealthy people. Over the years, they made very smart investments and created more wealth. They also lived through WWII. George served in the U.S. Army and was stationed as far away as India, while Virginia served in the American Red Cross in England.

Their estate in Chattanooga included a two story house, a two acre Japanese garden with two goldfish ponds, cherry trees, and dogwoods. Hidden paths wound through black-eyed Susans and Virginia Blue bells, to reveal an herb garden and a garden house. I grew up in that garden, but I could never keep a house plant alive even if my life depended on it. You either have a green thumb or you don't. My mother did.

She came into our lives in 1980, about one year after my mother had left her comfortable life in Manila. Our little family had gone from having everything to having very little. We lived at Mansion Hills Apartments in a second floor two bedroom unit with my cousin Susan. Susan was a nurse at Erlanger Hospital. She was in her twenties, single, and had a good job in America. Having her aunt and two small cousins living in her apartment was not a long-term solution for any of us. This tension finally boiled over one day. Mom packed us up, and we moved out of the apartment.

Mom was industrious. She sold Avon products to relatives and neighbors. She also convinced Father Rudisil at the Catholic Church, Sts. Peter and Paul, to let her clean the church and let us live in the children's nursery until she could find a place we could afford. My sister and I slept in the nursery cribs. For my little sister, it was fine, but I was about to begin second grade.

I was too big for the cribs, and it was very uncomfortable. We washed up in the bathroom sink in the nursery, and we ate many 56 cent Krystal hamburgers. We were, in essence, homeless. But that wouldn't be the case for long. Father Rudisil helped my mother find a small two bedroom house with an uneven foundation and drafty windows on Eleanor Street. It didn't have centralized heat or air, and we spent most of our time in the big bedroom with my mother, keeping cool with a window air conditioning unit in the summer and a space heater in the winter.

Mom had saved up three months of rent and grocery money. She needed to get a job before money ran out, a difficult thing to do in America without a high school diploma. Father Rudisil told my mother about a social worker named Charlotte Ramo who went to our church. He thought she might be able to help us. Charlotte worked for a nonprofit organization in downtown Chattanooga called Senior Neighbors of Chattanooga.

So one spring morning, we hopped on a CARTA bus transit to find Senior Neighbors in downtown Chattanooga.

Senior Neighbors had been founded in the 1970s to keep seniors active, social, and engaged in the community. They had a sewing circle and a theater program where the seniors would produce and perform plays. They also had dance classes and language classes. There was a cafeteria on site. The brick building had several ramps and hand rails throughout.

My mother had my sister and me in tow as we zigged and zagged up the front ramp of the building.

We found the front desk and Mom, with her thick Filipino accent announced, "Hello, my name is Priscila. I have an appointment with Miss Charlotte Ramo."

The receptionist, probably a fan of Farrah Faucet, had dark hair that was feathered and held in place with lots of hairspray. It was the perfect hairdo in 1980. She wore a plaid blouse, hoop earrings, and platform sandals, also indicative of the fashion transition between the late seventies and early eighties. She very kindly responded to my mother, "I'll see if she is in her office. If you'll have a seat on the bench, we will be right back."

The waiting area had a bench with hard leather and a droopy indoor plant in the corner. Mom had me sit on the end closest to the plant. She sat next to me and put my sister in her lap. Her purse, as always, was clutched tightly under her right arm. I looked up at the wall above the bench, and there was a portrait of a smiling woman at a ribbon cutting, probably for that very building. The woman had on a smart wool suit, a strand of pearls, a matching hat, and a very lady like smile. The little brass plaque on the portrait said, "Virginia Wing Power, Founder, Senior Neighbors of Chattanooga."

After a few minutes, a well-dressed older woman with platinum hair emerged from the offices in the back. She asked my mother, "Are you Priscila?"

My mother placed my sister on the bench next to me and stood up. "Yes, ma'am."

The woman extended her hand. "My name is Charlotte Ramo. Father Rudisil spoke very well of you."

My mother's shoulders relaxed. A broad smile spread across her face, and her eyes danced. "Oh, thank you." She was relieved to be recognized, and she felt this was a sign from God. And it was.

Charlotte asked, "Why don't you and your girls come into my office, and let's talk."

My mother took my sister's right hand and looked back at me, without saying a word. I knew she meant for me to stay close. I hopped off the bench with my little legs that had been dangling off the edge. I scurried behind my mother closely.

Charlotte's office was warm and inviting, but it didn't have any windows. She had macrame wall hangings made by the seniors to decorate her office. She had two guest chairs on the other side of her desk. My mother sat in one chair, and my sister and I shared the other chair. We were tiny girls and could fit in one chair.

Charlotte begins, "Priscila, do you mind if I ask how old you are?"

"I'm 42 years old."

"Well, that will be a challenge for us to provide you with services, because this organization serves seniors, and you are too young."

My mother responded quickly," But I don't need services. I need a job. I can type and will work very hard."

"Where did you go to school?"

My mother drooped a little, "Well, I went to school in the Philippines, but I did not finish high school. I learned how to type and do secretary work, and I got my beautician license in Manila. But I can learn to do anything."

"Well, I don't have anything for you here. But I might know someone who is looking for some help. It's a housekeeping job and a gardening job."

My mother sat up very straight, "I am a good gardener. In the Philippines, I had two big gardens."

"Can you write down your phone number? And I will call you tomorrow."

My mother had beautiful cursive penmanship, it was clear and delicate at the same time, the kind of handwriting you learn under the tutelage of Catholic nuns.

"Thank you, Miss Charlotte. Thank you for your help."

"You're welcome, Priscila. I will call you tomorrow."

We left the building. My mother clutching my little sister's right hand with her left hand, her purse under her right arm, and me following very closely. We walked one block to the bus stop and caught the CARTA bus back to our little rented house on Eleanor Street.

The next morning, the phone rang around 8:30 a.m. Miss Charlotte kept her promise.

"Hello, Priscila?"

"Yes, Miss Charlotte?"

"Good morning, Priscila. I've arranged a job interview for you with a woman named Ginny. I know you don't have a car, so do you mind if she picks you up?"

"Can I bring my girls?"

"Yes, that's fine. She knows you have two girls. She will be there at 10:00 a.m. Is that enough time for you to get ready?"

"Yes! We will be ready."

At 9:45 a.m., my mother, my sister, and I were sitting on our little porch. It was a bright spring day, not too hot, and not humid. Mom liked to dress Peachy and me alike. That day, we had on matching sandals from Woolworths, matching denim shorts and pink shirts.

At exactly 10:00 a.m., a 1971 Lincoln Continental in robin egg blue with a black top and suicide doors pulled up. In the back seat was a muscular, regal, pure bred Dalmatian dog. His spots were perfectly round and very black against the rest of his white coat. He didn't hang out the window like you would expect dogs to do, rather he sat still in the back seat by the window and looked straight ahead. He was guarding, calm and ready for whatever.

A petite white woman with gray, wavy, cropped hair, climbed out of the big car. She walked around the long nose of the car and toward the sidewalk. She wore a green blouse with a matching green and white print skirt from Talbot's. She had on canvas green flats, and she carried a wicker spring handbag with a leather strap and metal snap. We met her at the edge of the sidewalk. She extended her right hand and said in a melodic, southern accent, "Hello, my name is Virginia Wing Power, but people call me 'Ginny.'" Her name rang a bell with me and I realized she was the lady in the portrait in the waiting room, only she looked older than in the portrait. I immediately got the sense that she was important.

"Hello, Mrs. Power. I'm Priscila. These are my girls. The older one is Pinky, and the little one is Peachy."

She smiles at us and said, "Well, hello, girls." Then smiling at my mother again, "Well, shall we get going? I want to show you the house and garden."

My mother just nodded her head and nudged Peachy and me toward the car. But my sister and I were very reticent to get in the car. The dog was huge and scary.

Mrs. Power noticed and said, "Oh, that's Hero Two. He's very gentle. But if you are afraid of him, you can all sit in the front with me. The front seat is very roomy." The Powers had five generations of Dalmatians over the years. Being from the Greatest Generation who lived through WWII, their dogs' names had something to do with the war. The first Dalmatian was Colonel, the second was Hector, named after an army officer, then Hero One, and Hero Two. By the time the Powers passed away in the 1990s, there was a Hero Three, who was a rambunctious puppy who chewed everything and drove my mother crazy.

The front seat of that Lincoln Continental was indeed very roomy. The interior was robin egg blue, too, and the front seat was like a sofa with fine stitching. The car was impeccably clean. My mother sat in the middle, and Mrs. Power insisted she strap my sister and me in the seatbelt, which was a lap belt. It didn't have a shoulder strap. Mrs. Power was a small woman, and she could barely see over the giant steering wheel, but she handled that big luxury car just fine.

We drove two miles toward a very wealthy part of town

called Riverview. The neighborhood was near the Tennessee River and the Riverview Golf and Country Club. We took Riverview Road, a gently winding avenue with big houses on one side of the road and the golf course on the other. Their house was on a dead end street, tucked away behind ancient magnolia trees, which were in full bloom and incredibly fragrant. There was a gravel parking pad big enough for three cars in the front of the house.

At the front was a greenhouse full of lush plants. To the right of the greenhouse was the indoor car garage. And to the right of that were big stone, curved steps that led to the garden.

We climbed the stone steps, and when we reached the top, we were standing at a patio with an overhead trellis. It was covered with muscadine grape vines and honey suckle, creating a natural shade over the patio. Bumble bees would hover over the honeysuckle and move on. The air was still.

There was modest, but sturdy patio furniture. Mrs. Power invited my mother to have a seat and encouraged Peachy and me to play in the grassy area at the edge of the garden. But we wouldn't leave my mother's side.

"Do you like it here?"

"Yes, it's beautiful."

"I will need you at least three days a week. You will keep the house and tend to some of the garden. I have a gardener who does most of the landscaping, and my husband likes to cut the grass himself. He loves to ride the lawn mower. I will pay you $7.25 per hour, and you can bring your girls."

My mother agreed to the terms and worked for Mr. and Mrs. Power for twenty-seven years. What started out as three days per week became five days per week. What started out as cleaning and tending garden eventually included cooking, laundry, and ironing. My mother saved every penny and by

1981, she had enough money for a down payment for a small two-bedroom house on Hixson Pike, a main road by Riverview and walking distance from the Powers' house. The house was $25,000.

As a child, I would help in the garden by pulling weeds. Mrs. Power would give me 50 cents for helping and I used to put the quarters in a metal piggy bank. She would also give me a quarter whenever I used a four-syllable word. She would give me flash cards with big words on one side and the definition of the word on the back. She took my sister and me to the library and got us library cards so we would go to the children's section and read. She introduced me to Rudyard Kipling's *The Jungle Book.* My favorites were the Nancy Drew books and Hardy Boys books. In the summertime, Mrs. Power would read the *Tales of Mother Goose* to us every day. "There was an old woman who lived in a shoe. She had so many children she didn't know what to do…" always with the melodic southern accent.

I realized later that she read to us mainly for my sister, who was disabled by this time.

Virginia also used her good china and good silver every day. There was a big cabinet where all the silver was kept and I remember sometimes helping my mother polish the silver. Every piece of silver was engraved with a cursive "P" for the last name, Power. The china had a light gray scroll pattern and was very subtle. One day, Virginia said to me, "Pinky, let's teach you how to properly set a table."

For almost two hours, she showed me each piece of silverware and what it was used for. She showed me how to set the table, where to place the glasses, the forks, and spoons. She taught me how to place the napkin in my lap, and how to hold the utensils properly. I was getting a private Cotillion lesson.

When I was in the third grade, Mrs. Power asked my

mother, "Priscila, I notice Pinky really likes to dance. Would it be all right with you if I enrolled her in ballet lessons?"

My mother agreed, and I was giddy for a week. I remember my first ballet slippers. They were a size 1. I had two leotards, one light blue and one pink. I had two pairs of tights, one pink and one white.

Mrs. Power would pick me up from school every Tuesday afternoon at 3:30 p.m. and drive me to ballet lessons. She would wait in the waiting room for an hour and sometimes fall asleep and snore. At Christmas time, she would take my sister and me to see *The Nutcracker* at the Tivoli Theater. I would get home and dance in my room all night, pretending to be a ballerina. I have not seen *The Nutcracker* in years, because seeing it now would cause me to weep uncontrollably.

It was around Christmas time in my sixth grade year that Mrs. Power spoke to my mother in their big kitchen, "Priscila, George and I want to talk to you about something."

"Have I done something wrong?"

"No, not at all. Have a seat." They sat in the kitchen table.

She continued, "We know Peachy has limitations, but Pinky is very smart, and she has lots of potential. We would like to send her to Girls Preparatory School."

"But that's an expensive school. I can't afford that."

"We would pay her tuition. You would just have to worry about her uniforms, her books, and school supplies."

"But that is a school for rich girls, and we are poor. She won't fit in, and she will be left out."

"Priscila, she will learn to fit in. But she needs a good education. We will also pay for her to continue dance lessons and theater lessons. She needs to be a well-rounded lady."

"I don't know. Can I think about it over night? And I need to talk to Pinky."

I remember my mother was very quiet that evening. She

wasn't mad, just deep in thought. When she was mad, there would be a chill in the air. If she was sad, it would be raining. That night, the evening was very still, except for the sounds of the cogs of her mind churning.

After cleaning up from dinner, we sat in the dining room. She was at the end of the table toward the kitchen, and I was sitting on the other side of the table facing the dining room windows, which were blinking with Christmas lights. Mom loved Christmas and always over decorated. Eventually, the Christmas decorations just stayed up all year.

"Pinky, Mr. and Mrs. Power want to send you to GPS. What do you think about that?"

"The expensive school?"

"Yes."

"Why?"

"Because you're smart, and they think you need a good education."

"But we can't afford that."

"I know. They will pay for it."

I didn't know what to say, but I knew this was right. My instincts rarely failed me, and I always knew when something was right. It was a sensation in the pit of my stomach. It's the same satisfying feeling you get when you find the right puzzle piece to a complicated puzzle. You click it into place, and it fits so perfectly, you can feel the endorphins release in your brain. That's how I felt at that moment. But even as a child, I understood diplomacy.

I said to my mother, "What do you think, Mom?"

She moved her eyes to the center of the dining room table, and a deep furrow formed between her eyes. She waited a beat and said, "I'm scared for you."

"Why?"

My mother told me once I asked "why" questions so much

that one time she locked herself in the bathroom to get away from me. I love "why" questions.

"Because we are poor, and they will all be rich, and you might not fit in, and I don't want you to feel left out."

She had a good point. But my mind raced, and I thought to myself, *I was afraid of America, but I learned English and made friends at my other school. Why can't I make friends at this school?*

I said, "Don't be scared, Mom. I'm not scared. I can do it."

Mom shifted her gaze back to me. She traced my face with her eyes. Then she said, "You have to study and work hard. Don't waste their money."

"I won't. I promise."

The next day, my mother told Mrs. Power we would accept the offer. Mrs. Power smiled gently and said, "That's great news, Priscila. You are making the right decision."

I started GPS in the Fall of 1984 and graduated in Spring of 1990.

There is a photo of Mrs. Power and me, hanging on my wall of family photos. It was my senior year at GPS, and I had just finished my Chapel Talk. Every girl gives a speech to the entire student body during her senior year, and it trains the girls to write well and present in front of an audience. The girls can invite family and close family friends to attend their Chapel Talk. The family had a special section in the front to the left of the podium. And each family member was introduced by the headmaster to the entire student body. There was a special table in the rotunda of the school for the girl giving her Chapel Talk, and the table would have a guest book where anyone, including teachers and other girls, could write thoughtful and encouraging messages. There were several bouquets of flowers and balloons. Chapel Talk day was a special and important rite of passage.

In this photo, I was wearing my white uniform and the traditional black ribbon bow on the front. The iconic GPS uniform had not changed since the institution was founded in 1906. Mrs. Power had her arm around me and was wearing a light blue printed dress. She was in her eighties by then. When you hear my lilting southern accent, especially when I want to emphasize a thought, that is Virginia speaking.

Me with Ginny on Chapel Talk Day at
Girls Preparatory School, 1990.

CHAPTER 5

Agnes

During my sophomore year in high school, I met a boy who went to McCallie School, a boys' school at the other side of the Tennessee River. He was a boarding student from Memphis, Tennessee. There were three main private schools in Chattanooga: Girls Preparatory School for girls, McCallie School, and Baylor School, also for boys. The boy's name was Geoff, and he was an artist. I loved artists. Geoff looked like a young Richard Dreyfuss. He had blonde wavy hair, piercing blue eyes, and was the first boy to ever tell me I was beautiful. He was my first true love. Oh, how I loved that boy!

During my junior year, it was time to look at colleges, and GPS had a department dedicated to matching girls to colleges. One of the things they did was gauge a girl's interest in a college, find a GPS alum who graduated from that college or was currently enrolled, and arrange for the girl to meet the alum. The pipeline to college was sturdier than any metal girder of any bridge. Every girl was expected to have a college acceptance at graduation, so when they called out your name at the ceremony, they handed you your diploma and announced your college. The pressure and expectation to go to college was immense. There was no question that every girl had a future. While we think the "Future is Female" is a recent phenomenon, I have known this fact for quite some time.

One afternoon, after my last class of the day, I went to see the college counselor. Her office was located on the main hall of the main classroom building, down the hall from the English Literature classrooms. I have to admit, I loved my senior year in English class. The first semester was called "The Shakespeare Project" where we focused on *Hamlet* for an entire semester, memorizing passages, writing several papers (at least five) about Shakespeare and about the play. One of my favorite papers was about how our present-day language was derived from Shakespeare, like the phrase, "Every dog has his day."

The spring project was called "The Poetry Project." We picked any poet of our choosing, and we wrote one paper describing the poet. Then we dissected at least three poems, discussing not only the poems' verse configuration, what emotions the poems illicit, but also identifying the poet's voice and message he or she was trying to convey through writing.

This was only a sample of the academic curriculum at GPS. From seventh to twelfth grades, we also had extracurricular activities like sports and art. Needless to say, the families who sent girls to GP, got every penny's worth. Every girl was ready for the rigor of college upon graduation.

It was with a strong sense of confidence about academic preparedness that I went to see the college counselor. I honestly cannot remember her name, but I remember her office. It was a decent sized office with high ceilings and one tall window. It was decorated with posters from various colleges, including studies abroad. She had college brochures *everywhere*.

I wanted to talk to her about colleges in Memphis. I was in love! The counselor found an alumna at Rhodes College in Memphis, and we arranged for a college visit. Don't ask me how I managed to convince my mother to let me go, but she was in touch with the alumna's parents in Chattanooga, and they reassured her I would be fine.

Truthfully, I was more interested in seeing that boy more than the college. The GPS alum knew it. The Rhodes College counselor knew it. *Everybody* knew it, especially my mother and Mrs. Power. There was a lot of fighting and yelling leading up to the college visit.

Have you heard that phrase "Tiger Mom" to describe overprotective, Asian mothers? That would be an understatement to describe my mother during this time period. She said the rosary every night, begging God to protect my virtues, asking for divine intervention.

And intervene was exactly what God did. One day, Mrs. Power says, "Pinky, I'd like to show you my college in Atlanta, Agnes Scott. You might like it. There's a weekend coming up called Great Scott Weekend, and I'd like to take you."

We were standing in Mrs. Power's kitchen, and my mother was there. Without saying an audible word, my mother told me, "You will go. You do not have a choice."

But what about my boyfriend? I had to be with that boy! I was convinced that he was my one true love.

Not having a choice, I begrudgingly agreed to Great Scott Weekend.

So Mrs. Power, my mother, my sister, and I drove to Atlanta on a beautiful fall weekend. I felt like I had a cold. I took a lot of cold medicine and slept in the back seat during the two hour drive. It was more like two and half hours because Mrs. Power drove in the right lane at the exact speed limit, which was fifty-five miles per hour back then. I don't think young people today have any concept of just how slow things used to be. The only thing "instant" back then was ramen noodles. We didn't have cell phones. We didn't have social media with instant photos and videos. We were able to fully enjoy our youth, make our mistakes in a smaller community, and not have to weather "adultification" until much later.

I was curled up in the backseat of the big Lincoln Continental next to my sister, with my mother in the front seat, and Mrs. Power firmly gripping the mammoth steering wheel with her hands at 10 o'clock and 2 o'clock. The Lincoln was a smooth ride. But when we were approaching downtown Atlanta, my mother woke me up and said, "Pinky, wake up. We're almost there."

I sat up in the back seat and looked out the window. I saw, for the first time, the Atlanta skyline. Mrs. Power got off the highway at the Tenth Street exit. She drove us through Midtown Atlanta to the corner of Peachtree Street and Ponce de Leon Avenue in front of the Fox Theater. The Lincoln's left turn signal was a clear and precise tick-tick-tick-tick-tick. She turned left onto Ponce and headed east toward Decatur.

Even back then, there was so much to see on Ponce. The traffic slowed down, and it became more lush as we headed into Decatur. The trees were changing color, and slivers of sunshine pierced through the leaves and branches. Ponce de Leon was a winding road, and you didn't know what fall color would show up next around a bend. It was beautiful.

During that car ride, I had this overwhelming sense that I was going toward something. I still make this commute, and I still have this same feeling.

We arrived in Decatur and found our way to East College Avenue. We pulled into the front round about driveway of the college and found a visitor's parking spot in front of the college. The spot had a piece of paper taped to a cone that said,

"Reserved: Mrs. Wing-Power." Now, if that parking reservation was not an indicator of Mrs. Power's influence at the college, then I don't know what else could be.

The first building I saw was Rebekah Hall. There were large magnolia trees in front, and there was a wrap-around porch lined with white, wooden rocking chairs. There was a breezeway that connected Rebekah Hall to Main Hall, the oldest of the buildings on campus. And just beyond the breezeway was the front quad with the gazebo.

I got out of the car and set foot for the first time on campus. I thought, *Boyfriend? What boyfriend in Memphis?* I had already forgotten his name. I was in love all right, but it wasn't with a boy. It was with a place.

It was Great Scott 1989 and there were purple balloons and images of Scottie dogs everywhere. This weekend was special because it was also the centennial anniversary of the college. There were women of all ages and sizes everywhere. There were golf carts driving older alumnae throughout the college. I have recently found myself on one of these golf carts at an event on campus, and I love it!

All the paths connecting the buildings were red brick. On a rainy day, you would step on a loose brick, which had water underneath, and the brick would squirt rainwater up at you. Fun times.

After that weekend, I went back to GPS to finish high school and complete the application process for Agnes Scott. I was thrilled to get the acceptance letter in the mail, but frankly, I had already started packing because there was no doubt in my mind where I was going.

I started Agnes Scott in the fall of 1990. Mr. and Mrs. Power paid for college on one condition. I had to keep a 3.0 grade point average. I was *blessed.*

Back then, first year students had a curfew. If you weren't back in the dorm before midnight, you got locked out . . . and in trouble. Men were not allowed in the dorms, except for certain hours called parietals. During parietals, if you had a boyfriend, a brother, a father, or anyone of the male persuasion accompany you into the dorm, you yelled, "Man on the hall!!" at the top of your lungs as soon as the elevator opened, and you kept yelling it until you had him safely tucked away in your room. And if that boy had to pee, his poor soul had to hold it and make it to the gymnasium building or to one of the classroom buildings where there was a men's bathroom.

I believe our class was largely responsible for extending parietals from a few hours on certain days to overnight stays. Our argument was if the women who had single sex orientations were able to have girlfriends in the dorms at any time, then why couldn't the women who dated men be allowed more leniency? We straight girls felt discriminated against. How about that for challenging your sense of inclusion?

The 1990s at Agnes Scott can best be summarized as rigorous studies, of course, "Beverly Hills 90210" and "Melrose Place," Laura Ashley dresses, big hair bows and scrunchies, six-mile drives down Ponce de Leon toward Georgia Tech, and hidden beer. Lots of hidden beer.

But the most important thing about the college, and this speaks to the deepest and most ancient part of the college's culture, is the Honor Code. Every freshman class signs a contract with the college and pledges to uphold integrity and ethics. This happens in present day Agnes Scott. The contract is on a very large parchment paper with the Honor Code pledge, and every woman signs her name. The contract is framed and hung in Buttrick Hall, the main classroom building of the college. Students walk by it every single day and are reminded of living honorably. The Honor Code basically says, "No stealing. No cheating. No lying. And especially no plagiarizing." Stealing another person's ideas and words is a big no-no.

GPS had an Honor Code, as well. I have been conditioned to live with honor since the seventh grade.

With a college as old as Agnes Scott, there is so much history and so many tales, including ghost stories. I found the ghost stories to be entertaining and a charming part of the college history until one spring evening my junior year.

As a theater major, I spent most of my time in the Dana Fine Arts Building. This building was designed by famous Atlanta architect, John Portman, and dedicated in 1965. Dana had all arts courses, including visual arts, theater, and mixed media. As a theater major, I also had to take other forms of arts classes including visual fine arts.

In the spring semester of my junior year, I had a major visual art project due as part of my final. I recall working in charcoal and newsprint paper. I was working late in one of the second level art classrooms, hunched over a large drafting table, my hands blackened from the charcoal. The sun had gone down almost two hours prior. I missed dinner at the dining hall, but I was determined to finish that project, because I had two more papers to write before the semester was over. Time was of the essence. Besides, I had some instant ramen I could heat up for dinner back in the dorm.

The overhead light of the classroom flickered for a quick second. I ignored it. Then I heard a shuffling noise in the hall. I thought, *Oh, the cleaning crew is here. It's late and about that time. Someone should be here in a moment to take the trash.* With that thought, I started gathering my discarded newsprint and stuffing it into the one trash can in the classroom by the door so the janitor could take the trash.

I went back to the drafting table and shook a new charcoal stick out of the box, then continued working on the newsprint. I do not remember what the art piece looked like or what it was about, and frankly, it does not matter.

I had on jeans, sneakers, and a light sweater. Even though it was spring, it was early in the season, and there was still a slight chill in the air.

I heard shuffling in the hall again. I was sure that sound was the rolling wheels of the janitor's big pushcart. I mean, I *firmly* believed this.

I expected to see the janitor in the doorway of the classroom any moment, but no one came. Then I heard music in the building.

I thought it was odd, because there were no rehearsals going on. There was no play in production at that time.

So I walked out into the hall, looking for the source of the music. The impulse to follow it was powerful and irresistible. I suddenly felt a chill in the hall. I ignored it because of the changing weather and the fact that the sun had gone down.

I kept listening and determined the music was coming from the first level, where the theater classrooms were located. I went downstairs.

There was a long, slowly graded ramp that led from the main hall of the building into the theater side of the building. The doors to the front of the theater were on the left, and just a few feet from there was the door leading to the back of the theater. Last, beyond that door, was a rehearsal classroom.

In that classroom, I found the source of the music. It was a radio, a clock radio, that was used as a prop. The bright red digits of the clock radio were blinking off and on, and it was on an oldies station playing a song from the 1970s. There was no one in the room. I walked to the radio. I pushed the off button a couple of times, but it wouldn't turn off. I grabbed the cord and followed it with my hand with the intention of unplugging it. But when I found the other end of the cord, I realize it wasn't even plugged in. There wasn't even a plug behind the table.

Just then, I felt someone standing behind me. I jerked my head up and whipped around.

There, standing in the doorway, was a young woman with very long, brown hair parted down the middle. She had brown eyes and thin lips. She wore bell bottom jeans, platform sandals, and a light-colored blouse with an empire waist. She had on a braided necklace with some kind of pendant.

She calmly turned around and walked back into the hall.

I said, "Uh, hey..."

I followed her into the hall, but there was no one there. Scurrying to the backstage door then back into the main hall, I still saw no one there. I was spooked to death. So I hurried back to the second floor to the visual art classroom, and quickly stuffed my things into my back pack. Trembling, I fished my dorm key out of the front zipper pocket and made a fist around it with the key poking out between my middle finger and pointer finger. I was ready to use it as a weapon if I needed to defend myself. We had learned this in self-defense class during my freshman year.

I hightailed it out of the building, taking in quick breaths and blowing air through my gritting teeth.

I darted out of the building into the dark and cut through the back quad, in desperate need to find a well-lit area of the campus. I started out in a brisk walk, escalated my steps, and by the time I reached the front quad, near the gazebo, I was fully sprinting. Scared as hell. When I reached my dorm room,

I turned on every single light and left them on all night. I slept with the lights on.

Later, and I don't know exactly when, I heard a story about a young woman in the 1970s who was working on pottery in the arts building one night. The fast spinning of the potter's wheel caught her long dark hair and snapped her neck.

Even as I write this, it gives me chills.

Too much happened in my four years at Agnes Scott for me to document, and so much happened that particular spring. Upperclassmen were assigned a freshman little sister to help the new student acclimate to college. My little sister was Vivi, who grew up on a ranch and had a Texas drawl and authentic cowboy boots. Although her name was Vivi, I called her "Kiwi," because she was a fuzzy girl. She was pretty, but she had to shave all the time. Her roommate, Allison, also became one my closest friends. Allison was from Houston, Texas and danced with the Houston Ballet. She was tall, slender, and floated like a gazelle. The first time we met was in the Alston Student Center, and she had a case of "RBF," or Resting Bitch Face. I was sure that it was all or nothing with Allison. We were either going to get along or hate each other. We hit it off swimmingly.

Kiwi's parents gave her a car, which was a white 4 door sedan of some sort with dark tinted windows. This made sense for a young woman from Texas, since a white vehicle reflected the heat of the sun, and dark tinted windows would keep the interior cooler.

The dark tinted windows became a crucial part of our survival one Friday night when Kiwi and I set out down Ponce de Leon toward Georgia Tech, with plans to attend a fraternity party.

As we approached Atlanta and downtown, we noticed

the traffic was getting thicker and thicker. We didn't think too much of it. It was a Friday night in Atlanta, and more traffic was normal. Kiwi made a left on a side street to get off Ponce and catch North Avenue toward Georgia Tech. We arrived at the corner of North Avenue and Peachtree Street, and there it was. *Freaknik 1993.*

If you have not heard about Freaknik or don't know what it was like in 1993, Google it.

Kiwi's left hand immediately went to the console of her driver's side door, and I heard the "thud" sound of the doors locking.

There were black people everywhere. Hanging on the street, hanging out of cars, dancing on the hood of the cars, loud hip-hop music going *boom-tish, boom-boom-tish, boom-tish, boom-boom-tish.* I thought I saw Salt-n-Pepa cross the street three times.

I was in my early twenties, and I had never been through Al Vivian's Diversity & Inclusion Training (which I have now done nine times). And keep in mind, I grew up in Chattanooga and went to an all-girls prep school, where there was not much diversity. This memory of how I felt is one of the reasons I am glad today that my son attends a charter school in the city with a majority black population. I do not want him to be afraid of black people.

I said to Kiwi, "What on earth?!"

She said, "I don't know! But remain calm."

We could not turn around; there were cars behind us. The only thing we could do was go straight and cross the intersection. It took us almost two hours to cross that intersection, and her tinted windows saved our asses. Imagine, if you can, two Agnes Scotties, one from Texas and the other Filipino, smack dab in the middle of Freaknik.

The Freaknik of the 1990s ensued all kinds of laws. The

city was getting ready for the Olympics, and they were just not going to put up with any of it. Nope. There are still "No cruising" signs and ordinances up and down Peachtree Street.

But honestly, Freaknik was part of the Atlanta journey and part of its beautiful grit. The city is trying to sanitize itself now, and I'm a little sad about it, like when NCR made the Cheetah Strip Club take down its famous sign because they did not want to be reminded the new corporate headquarters was across the street from a high-end strip club. Or when people were outraged when the Atlanta United Soccer team took their MLS Cup after the parade to Magic City, a strip club on the Southside of town. If it didn't end up at Magic City, it would have ended up at The Clermont Lounge, the other strip club on the north end of town. I felt sorry for the intern who had to try to get all the glitter and baby oil off that MLS Cup. Embrace the strip clubs, folks.

Kiwi and I survived Freaknik 1993. She and I finally made it to Georgia Tech, a bit shaken, but all in one piece. Our two guy friends at the Tech fraternity let us sleep in their bunk beds, and they took the couches in the recreation room. They were also nice enough to guard the bathroom door when we washed up the next morning before heading back to campus.

The ghost story, partying at Tech, and accidentally walking into Freaknik are not Agnes Scott to me. Agnes Scott was the beginning of my love for Atlanta and is actually a lifetime of friendships, the constant search for learning and reaching beyond, and most importantly, a deep sense of belonging to something greater than myself.

The college ring is a black onyx with antique engraving. On one side of the ring is engraved the college year graduation and the other side is "BA" for my Bachelors. Inside the ring are my initials, "MLB."

Scotties are also known as "The Black Ring Mafia."

Scotties are strong, innovative, curious, hardworking, and have unmovable integrity. When I am facing any challenge, especially one of intellect or leadership, I wear my ring. It grounds me, and reminds me of who I am.

"The Future is Female." Tell me something I don't already know.

Agnes Scott College Class of 1990 on our 25th Reunion, April 2019.

PART 2

The Men

CHAPTER 6

Loreto

My father, Loreto, was born on March 18, but I don't know the year. I remember he was slightly younger than my mother. I also vividly remember Dad's love of Elvis, and how much he emulated the King of Rock. In the late 1960s and early 1970s, Dad wore a lot of pomade in his hair and managed to comb a perfect pompadour with a bit of the Superman curl over his forehead—so Elvis! He also wore skinny leg shark skin trousers and a gold chain. Dad was suave.

Dad was from the part of the Philippines called Ilocos, a northern region of the big island, Luzon. Ilocos was first inhabited by the aboriginal peoples, the Negritos. They are known for their very dark brown skin and very thick hair. Their dialect was completely different from the dialect spoken in my mother's province of Bulacan.

My grandmother on my father's side was known as "Mamang," and the grandmother on my mother's side was called "Inang." My mother did not get along well with Mamang, as I recall, because Mamang had been married a couple of times and had children by more than one man. My mother, the former nun, judged her for it.

We visited Ilocos a few times in my early childhood, and mostly when my great-grandfather, "Tatang," was still alive. Tatang was ancient and his eyes were the glassy, gray eyes of very old people. He was thin and frail, but still with a thick head of very white hair. My mother loved Tatang, as she had a strong love for the elders of the family. She convinced my dad to bring Tatang back home with us to Manila so we could take care of him until he died. Dad agreed. Tatang is buried in our family cemetery in Manila.

My fondest memory about Tatang has to do with indoor plumbing. We had showers in our bathrooms at our house in Manila. He had never had a shower before, and he laughed and laughed so much with joy that rain could come out of a spicket from the wall. It made my mother happy to know we were able to bring Tatang so much joy toward the end of his life. He died before my sister was born.

Ilocos had beautiful beaches lined with palm trees and coconut trees. My teenage boy cousins on my father's side in the province would tie a machete around their waists, use a leather belt strap or a really strong rope, loop it around the trunk of the coconut tree and use it to leverage their weight and climb the coconut trees. When they got to the top, they would hold on to the strap with one hand, and use the other hand to chop down the coconuts with the machete. The coconuts would land softly in the sand with a muffled *thud*.

Then they would scurry down from the tree faster than when they climbed, gather the coconuts, and chop them open one at a time. I would drink fresh coconut juice right out of the shell. But the best was the fresh seafood. Seafood in the Philippines went from the ocean, into the fishing baskets, and right to the fire or outdoor grill. Oh, it was so good!

When I was about 3 years old, we were visiting Ilocos and spending the day at the beach. The ocean was turquoise blue, the sun clear and bright, and the sand a perfect contrast to the blue sky and ocean. It seemed like a vacation ad. We had our big blankets and picnic baskets nestled under a leaning palm tree and the crashing sounds of the waves were steady and soothing. My father decided to go for a swim and take me with him.

As he waded into the ocean, the waves got taller and taller. I was frightened by their power, by the strong seaweed, and the salty smell of the ocean. My father had a good grip on me. He had me pressed up against his chest and he was jumping up with the crest of the waves. But regardless of his good grip, I was scared to death.

I screamed, "Aaah! Aah! Tatay, no! Aah! Nanay, help me! Help me!"

My mother was on the shore, her light cotton dress billowing and her hair blowing to one side with the breeze. She flapped her arms and yelled at my father, "Loreto! Come back! Bring her back, right now!"

"She'll be fine!" he yelled back.

"No! No! She is scared to death. You bring her back right now!"

Now I was terrified by the ocean and also by all the yelling between my parents.

My father relented and waded back toward the shore. My mother stood on the shore with the ocean lapping at her feet and ankles. As my father was climbing out of the water, my mother's arms were extended, anxious to clutch me. I had a high-pitched toddler's scream, and tears saltier than the sea were rolling down my face.

"My baby!" my mother exclaimed, taking me quickly out of my father's arms. She bounced me up and down and patted me on the back to calm me.

She then cussed out my father in Tagalog. He didn't say

much, as he was just trying to show me the beauty of the ocean. He didn't anticipate that it would frighten me so much.

Mom calmed me down, and pretty soon I fell asleep on the blanket under the tree. Wisps of my hair tickled my cheek, and the rhythm of the ocean coming and going continued. How is it that the ocean that frightened me so much was also soothing and lulling me to sleep?

That memory is the reason I am still afraid of water. I have waded into the ocean on occasion during beach vacations in my adult life, but honestly, I don't like it. I don't like the sand and don't like the ocean, but I love the beach! It's peculiar. I feel the beach is more of a state of mind than a place.

I was never mad at my father for taking me into the ocean; I was just scared. From what I can recall about my father, he did his best to be a good father and tried to be a good family man. One of his favorite things to do was to give gifts.

When I was almost five years old, my father came home one day and said, "I have something for you."

He pulled a little velvet box from his pocket. Inside were lovely pearl earrings with fourteen karat gold posts.

My mother was not pleased. "Loreto! What are you doing giving her such expensive gifts at this age! That is a waste!"

My father didn't say anything. He just held a sly grin on his face. Giving gifts was his love language. Dad didn't like to use words to express his love.

I happily took the little velvet box and ran off to the front garden to marvel at my new present, evading my mother's protest. Even as a child, I knew when something was expensive.

Somehow, one of those little earrings ended up in my nose. Young children sometimes shove things into their ears and noses to test the boundaries of physiology. That's just what I did.

First, I got the *slap-slap-slap* of the *chinela*. Then my mother wrangled the driver and grabbed her purse. We all piled into one of the cars and rushed to the hospital. The driver drove as fast as he could in Manila traffic, which was not very fast. There was so much honking. So much honking.

My mother briskly walked the hall of the hospital with a firm grip on my wrist. When we got to the counter, which I can only assume was the emergency room check-in, she spoke very fast and with a great sense of urgency. We didn't wait very long. I guess a small child with a pearl earring up her nose was, in fact, an emergency.

I recall sitting on the edge of the examining table, feeling the cold of the metal edge on the back of little brown, dangling, skinny legs. The doctor used a long tweezer-like instrument, carefully trying to pry the pearl earring out of my nostril. He mumbled under his breath, carefully fishing, until finally he said excitedly, "Gotcha!"

He carefully balanced the pearl earring in between the prongs of the tweezers, slowly turned around, and presented it to my mother.

She reached up, plucked the earring with two fingers and dropped it in her purse, simultaneously setting her jaw tight. She was mad. She was grateful to the doctor, but she was really mad at my father.

My mother was silent in the car ride home from the hospital.

When we arrived home, my father was having his afternoon *merienda* in the eating area of our outdoor kitchen at the back of the house. *Merienda* is Tagalog for the late afternoon snack before dinner, but it's basically a second lunch.

My mother walked into the kitchen area, clutching her purse. She brought a frigid chill to the room, frightening away the heat and humidity of the islands.

She did not say a word, but my father knew he was in trouble. She turned around and headed upstairs to the master suite. My father got up off the wood bench and followed her.

The door was closed, but my parents had a bad argument about what happened.

"Think, Loreto, think! You cannot give a four-year-old expensive pearl earrings!"

"Why, not?! It made her happy. I want to make her happy."

The cook and the nanny kept me with them in the back kitchen. One of the windows to the master suite was open, and my parents' arguing voices floated down into the garden.

That was a long afternoon, as I recall. My mother eventually forgave my father about the earrings, but it took a few days of the silent treatment. My mother had an iron will, and she could go days without speaking to you if she was mad at you. Days!

A couple of years later, when Peachy was almost two and I was six, my sister and I would eagerly wait for our father to come home from work every day. He came home around six o'clock, and dinner was usually at seven o'clock. That hour in between his arrival from work and dinner was our time with him.

Peachy and I would sit on the stone wall in the front garden like little brown sentinels. We would gaze toward the end of the block, keeping an eye out for my father's red Mustang.

When he rounded the corner and slowly drove down the block toward our house, we would hop off the wall and run to the garage to wait for him.

My father always brought home treats for us. He would bring us fresh fruit, Hershey's candy bars (which were a big deal in Manila), or *chicle*, Tagalog for gum. But the best part was when he would put me and my sister in the front seat of his Mustang to go for a ride. He would put my sister in the passenger side, and he would place me in his lap. He let me put my hands on the steering wheel then placed his big hands over mine to help me steer. We would circle the block.

My father also got involved in his community. He was the president of the neighborhood association at Silvina Village, and he sponsored the neighborhood basketball team. He loved basketball. In fact, most Filipinos love basketball. We are the shortest people in the world, but we love basketball. We also love boxing. One of the most historical occasions for the Philippines was the final boxing match between Muhammad Ali and Joe Frazier in 1975, also known as "The Thrilla in Manila." Ali won that fight on a technical knockout. That boxing match brought global attention to the Philippines. The two sports rivaled each other in popularity.

Every year, there was a basketball tournament with leagues from different neighborhood developments. Our league always made it into the championship game. There was something ethically questionable about the referees. Like the Filipino cops, a little *suhol* (bribe money), went a long way with referees.

To kick off the championship game, the neighborhood would throw a fiesta and parade for the team. The team would march in the parade in their basketball uniforms, sponsored by "LFB & Company," my father's business. There were children and music everywhere. As the boss's daughter, I was "Silvina Village Little Miss," and I had a satin ribbon sash I would wear in the parade with a little tiara. My dad would tightly clutch my little hand, and we would parade around a three-block radius to the neighborhood park where the basketball court was waiting with more children and more families. The fact that I wore a satin sash and a little crown in a parade when I was a small child comes as no surprise to people who know me now. In fact, it explains a lot.

Those early years of my childhood are such fond memories. We were all happy, especially my mother. But all of that happiness was shattered the day the letter arrived from Gloria, confessing her love affair with my father. That letter changed everything. My mother used to say that Gloria didn't have to tell her about the affair. My mother felt that ignorance was bliss. She said Gloria was jealous of our family. Gloria knew that my father was never going to leave his family for her, and that infuriated her.

My mother's heartbreak was deep and cavernous, and it echoed inside of her for almost three decades. It's hard to know what caused my father to stray. In a culture like the Philippines, men with money and power—even a little bit of power—must be intoxicating, and the temptation is great. My Dad was human and not infallible. But I know he tried, and he tried hard. He fought for my mother and tried to keep his family together, but my mother's deep Catholic faith was immense.

Sometime in the 2000s, long after my father was dead, and my mother, my sister, and I had been living in America for over twenty years. Mom made a decision to forgive my father. She had the priest at our church in Chattanooga say three masses for him. Then one day, she called me.

"Pinky, this is Nanay."

"Hi, Mom. What's up?"

"I'm going back to the Philippines in August. I'm going to get your father and bring him here to America."

"What do you mean you're going to get Dad and bring him here? He's dead and buried in Ilocos!"

"I know. I've made arrangements to have him exhumed, then cremated, and then I'm going to bring him back here. I have forgiven him, and he should be with our family."

My jaw dropped. But what can you say to Cila? When Cila makes up her mind about something, that's the end of it.

"Okay, Mom. How long will you be gone?"

"I'll go back for a month and a half. I'll be back with your father."

Then she hung up. Just like that.

A few weeks after this phone call, my mother and my sister went back to Manila. They were gone for most of August and early September. I was married to Tony at this point, and when she and my sister returned from Manila, Tony and I drove up to Chattanooga to meet them at the airport. It was a cool Saturday in September.

Tony and I met them at the gate, and I remember Tony's reaction when he saw my mother at the airport that day. Among many great things in Manila are the affordable services. For example, dental care is much cheaper in the Philippines, and so are cosmetic services. During that trip back to Manila, my mother decided to get her eyebrows darkened and had them tattooed. Well, it was not a great job. Tony said, "Oh, my God. Why does your mother look like the Joker?"

I punched him in the ribs and said, "Shut up! Don't let her hear you say that! Act like it looks good."

When my mother and sister deplaned, we hugged them, took the carry-on luggage from my mother, and then moved on to baggage claim and customs to claim the big boxes from Manila. We got a big cart and hauled all the boxes and luggage to the parking lot.

When we were loading the trunk, I said, "Hey, Mom, so... where's Dad?"

With her purse tightly clutched under her right arm, she pointed with her left hand at the box Tony was holding. The rectangular box was only about 15 pounds. Tony had both of his hands under the box cradling it and was just about to put it in the trunk when Mom said, "He's in that box."

Tony's eyes got very big as he realized he was holding a box with my father's remains. He quickly put the box in the trunk of the car and shivered.

I said, "Mom, how did you get Dad's remains through customs? Don't you need some paperwork or something?"

She says, "Oh, I'm not going to bother with any of that. I just didn't tell them those were your father's remains. And I'm not going to pay any additional fees to bring home my husband."

I asked, "Well, do you have him in an urn in that box?"

"No. He's in a big Ziploc bag inside an empty tub of 'I Can't Believe It's Not Butter.'"

Tony and I just stood there, staring, and at the same time, not at all surprised by Cila.

Tony and I headed back to Atlanta later that evening after getting Mom and my sister settled at home. The following Monday, I started researching online for urns for my father's remains. I really wanted to get my father out of the tub of fake butter. I found one for about $118, and then I called my mother.

"Mom, I found an urn for dad for about $118."

She replies, "Oh, don't waste your money, I already took care of that."

"What do you mean? I wanted to buy the urn for Dad."

"We were at TJ Maxx, and I saw something on sale, and it looked pretty good. So I bought it."

"You bought Dad's urn from TJ Maxx?! Mom, are you kidding me?!"

She was absolutely serious. The urn was actually very nice. My Dad is buried in it with my sister at our family cemetery in Chattanooga.

I really love TJ Maxx, because I can find great fashion deals. But I also go to TJ Maxx to mourn my father. After all, why does mourning have to occur by a graveside or at the cemetery? Mourning can happen anywhere.

Loreto holding me the day they
adopted me. Manila, 1971.

CHAPTER 7

George

G eorge, the man I refer to as my grandfather, was Virginia's husband. He was kind, yet firm and stern. He was also a strategic and wildly successful businessman. Already quite wealthy by the time we met them in 1980, the Powers were a vibrant and active couple in their seventies. I have, hanging in my living room, a beautifully framed photo of them canoeing in Wyoming on a camping trip in the late 1980s. The photo is one my most prized possessions.

George served in the Army during World War II. He was deaf in one ear thanks to a grenade. When you talked to him, he would turn his head so that his good ear was facing toward you, and he would listen as intently as possible.

Sometime in the early 1980s, we were celebrating Christmas at their house with their extended family. It was Christmas Eve, and Mom had been in the kitchen all day long. The smells of turkey and stuffing floated all throughout the big house. There were poinsettias everywhere, both red and white. There was garland draped on the front steps of the house and a fresh pine tree wreath on the front door. A fire was burning in the fireplace with the Dalmatian dog, Hero Two, cozy and curled up in front of it. There was a collection of Santa Clauses from their travels all over the world displayed on top of the grand piano. Opposite stood a ten-foot Christmas tree in front of the windows facing the side patio and the front of the house.

We had popped popcorn all day, and we were using a thread and needle to string it together so we could hang it on the tree. This was so much fun and kept my sister and me occupied all day long.

Virginia, having given me private cotillion lessons, allowed me to help set the dinner table. There was an Advent wreath as a center piece, with four slender candles. We used the Christmas place mats. The silver was polished, the good Waterford crystal on the table, and the good china with the subtle gray scroll was laid out. The table was set for sixteen.

To say the least, it was a beautiful Christmas. I was overjoyed. There were lots of presents under the tree. Lots of presents!

Around mid-afternoon, George walked into the kitchen and asked my mother, "Priscila, do you have a moment? I want to speak to you about something."

My mother stopped what she was doing at the sink and dried her hands with a drying cloth from the rack. She walked over to the kitchen table, where George was standing with a copy of The Wall Street Journal folded in half.

"Priscila, do you know what The Wall Street Journal is?"

Mom shrugged, "I sort of do. I know it is a newspaper, and you read it every day with your coffee and breakfast."

"Yes. It is the business newspaper. Let me show you." He opened it up and showed her the articles and the columns of stock initials and points. "You see these stocks? And you see how the points have gone up?"

"Yes. What are those stocks?"

"These are the stocks for Exxon and Dixie Yarns."

"Are those good stocks?"

"They are doing very well right now. But the stock market is a long game. Do you know what I mean by that?

"No."

"You have to watch these numbers and watch who is in charge of the country. It determines how these numbers go up and down. And these points are money. Each point is worth a dollar value. Now that Ronald Reagan is President, we should see better results."

"Okay. Thank you, for showing this to me, Mr. Power. I kind of understand, I think, but I need to learn more."

"Yes, Priscila, I plan to teach you more."

With that, George folded up the paper and left the kitchen. My mother went back to the counter and started placing trivets on the table so she could take the food out of the oven. We were eating buffet style.

About forty-five minutes later, my mother announced that the food was ready. Everyone gathered in the kitchen, and George began carving the turkey. Everyone had a plate and stood in line to get a piece of turkey, then fill their plates with stuffing and other sides.

I remember minding my manners at the table and doing my best to remember how to cut my food. I took small, lady like bites, exactly how Virginia taught me to do.

The dinner conversation was lively. I was asked about school, what my favorite subjects were, and about my dancing and ballet lessons. I talked about my reading list at school and how much I was enjoying the books about Jeeves, the British butler. It felt good being able to carry on conversations with adults.

After dinner, it took about thirty minutes to clear the table and clean up. My mother brewed coffee and set out the desserts. There was a chocolate cake, homemade apple pie, and homemade cherry pie.

I was just beside myself! I don't know if I was more excited about dessert or opening presents. The feeling of overwhelming happiness must have been all over my face, because the adults kept patting me on the back and giving me little hugs. My sister and I were the only children at this Christmas Eve dinner. George and Virginia never had children of their own, and the family seemed glad that we were there.

Dessert and coffee would wait for after the presents, which was just fine with me. I was getting both. As we gathered in the living room, every sitting chair and both couches had a person sitting in them. My sister and I sat on the floor, next to Hero Two. The fire was cracking under the mantle, which was decorated with red and gold garland. It took a moment for Hero Two to settle down. He knew there was a lot of excitement, and his whole body wagged. And I know dogs can smile, because Hero Two was smiling. His tail was a long, strong whip. It would wag quickly like a windshield wiper, or it would be straight and pointed when he was on alert mode. Pure bred Dalmatians are known for their alert stance and pointed tails. This is one reason fire departments are historically known to have Dalmatians.

Mom got a couple of large garbage bags to collect any torn paper or discarded ribbon. There wasn't that much trash, looking back on it. We were all very careful to open the wrapping and not squish the bows. George and Virginia survived the Great Depression, and there was a tacit understanding with everyone not to be wasteful.

My sister and I got toys, a few stuffed animals, games, some apparel items, and a few envelopes with $5, $10, $20 bills. We racked up!

George leaned over to my mother and handed her three white envelopes. Sitting at my mother's feet, I heard him quietly say, "Priscila, this is for you and the girls."

My mother reticently took the envelopes and asked, "What is this, Mr. Power?"

"Just open it, Priscila. It's from Ginny and me."

She carefully opened one of them.

Inside were stock certificates to Exxon Mobil. The next envelope held stock certificates to Dixie Yarns. The third envelope had a check. I don't know for how much.

My mother blinked, and her eyes became glassy and misty. I knew she wanted to weep, but pride kept it at bay. She turned to George and in a hoarse whisper said, "Oh, no, no, Mr. Power, I cannot take this. This is too much!"

She tried to hand him the envelopes back. She was demurring, grateful, shy, and prideful all at the same time, which is particularly Asian behavior.

George put his hand over my mother's hand and pushed the envelopes back. "Yes, Priscila, these are for you and the girls. Accept our gift. We love you all very much."

My mother surreptitiously wiped away a tear. She realized I was sitting on the floor, watching the whole thing. She put her hand on my left shoulder, and looked at my whole face. Then her eyes traced all around me, as if she was looking at me and the aura around me. It was as if she was looking into a crystal ball at my future. I knew I should sit very still. She looked over at my sister to my right and couldn't reach her with her hand, but I know she was hugging us both with all her being.

After a slow breath, Mom relaxed her shoulders. The corners of her mouth lifted. Turning back to the rest of the room, she re-engaged with the party and said, "Oh, dessert! I will go and slice up the cake and pies!"

She clutched the envelopes in her right hand as she stepped over my sister and me. She would tuck them safely into her purse.

I studied my grandparents, sitting in their matching yellow suede chairs with serene countenances, watching the Christmas scene.

Hero Two got up and navigated the piles of paper and

ribbon. He circled once and then settled in a perfect spiral at George's feet, as if to say to his master, "You have done a good job, Boss. I'm here for you."

I remember thinking as a child, *Wow. Why do they look so...calm and in control? Solid and unmovable? How can I be like that when I grow up?*

Those Christmas gifts paid for my down payment on my first condo a few years after I graduated from college, and for my first car. Mom did learn how to interpret *The Wall Street Journal*, and she would read the paper mid-morning after George had left for his office, which he did every day until well into his eighties.

About eight or nine years after that Christmas, George and Ginny would pay for my full tuition at Agnes Scott College. They never asked too much of my family. They appreciated the work my mother did for them, and eventually, Mom did almost everything at the house and garden. Their only expectations of me were to make good grades, be a gracious lady, use my education, and serve my community. I try to live up to that expectation every day.

George and Ginny on a camping
trip in Wyoming circa 1982.

CHAPTER 8

Sam

Agnes Scott women are also called "Scotties." During my sophomore year at college, it was time to declare a major. That was more than twenty-five years ago, so I don't know when Scotties have to declare a major now, but that was when we did it. At Thanksgiving, I was at home with my family for the break. I told my mother I wanted to major in Theater.

First, her eyes got very big. Her jaw set in tight, and her lips pursed just ever so slightly. A sudden chill came into the room, as if a giant freezer door was opened and you could feel the regular warmth of the room behind you, but cold air in front of you. This sensation of matriarch power has been perfected by Asian mothers over thousands of years. I have also learned this posture.

She finally growled, "No."

"Why? It's what I love. I want to do what I love."

"You want love, or do you want to eat? I will give you love. But you have to learn how to eat. No."

I honestly didn't agonize much. I had a back-up plan. I knew my mother well, and I knew she had always only entertained my love for the arts as a hobby.

I went back to school after the break, and I started the process for a dual degree in Theater and Spanish. My college advisors were Dudley Sanders and Dr. Rafael Ocasio. I lined up an internship in two places: The Latin American Association (LAA), and one at a theater lighting and production company. The executive director of the Latin American Association at the time was Maritza Soto Keen. The woman who hired me for the internship was Sara Gonzalez, God rest her soul. The theater production company was owned by Scott Ross.

After I did all that, I called my mother.

"Mom, I'm going to double major in Theater and Spanish, and I have internships in both. The Latin American Association will offer me a job after graduation."

Silence. Then, "Okay. Do you want adobo chicken when you come home for Christmas?" That was a green light. When Mom moved on to food, it was always a good sign.

I did my internships my junior year and started my part time job at the LAA my senior year.

The LAA had recently moved into a new building on Buford Highway in an area now known as Brookhaven. Maritza Keen was an incredibly capable executive director and took the organization to the next level. Before they were in that building, they were on the first level of a shopping center. The new building was across the street from an authentic Mexican restaurant called Panchos and down the road from the Havana Sandwich Shop. The black beans and rice, Cuban sandwiches, and fried plantains at Havana was the best kept secret in Atlanta. In fact, Buford Highway in general was a secret asset, at a time in Atlanta where "diversity" was just about black people and white people. Now this area is referred to as "Bu-Hi," and there's a website called "I love Bu-Hi." Good secrets are hard to keep secret forever. A lot has changed in Atlanta in twenty-five years. Or has it? I think so.

It was in that building that I found myself working on the second floor for the job development department of the LAA. Our department's role was to connect Hispanics to jobs, help them with worker's comp issues, and administer job training.

Our department was down the hall from Maritza's office. One day, I was standing in the hallway, talking to Claudia, the office manager.

I felt a stare. It was Martiza's, and I looked down the hall at her. She said, "Maria, can you come into my office for a minute? I need to talk to you."

The executive director just called me into her office. I thought, "Holy shit. Am I in trouble?" As I mentioned before, "Am I in trouble?" was a common question for me. I got in trouble a lot. I used to drive the nuns in Catholic school crazy. The ruler across my knuckles couldn't stop me from talking too much or asking too many questions all the time.

I traversed the hallway to her office, which was only about twenty feet, but seriously, it felt like a mile. My heart raced, and my stomach felt tight.

I walked into her corner office, and she was already seated in her chair. With windows on both sides, the colors were bright. It was just like the décor of the rest of the building, which was a reflection of Hispanic culture—bright, vibrant, soulful, and cheerful.

She said, "Please sit."

I sat across from her in one of the contemporary black chairs in front of her desk.

"How are you enjoying your internship?"

"I love it. I'm learning a lot."

"What are you learning?"

"I'm learning about how to help people find jobs. And I like how I can speak Spanish every day."

"That's great to hear." She shifted gears, "Listen, I want to tell you about an opportunity. One of our board members, Sam Zamarripa, is starting a public affairs firm, and he needs an assistant. I want to recommend you for the job. Are you interested?"

Oh, I wasn't in trouble.

"Uh, yes, of course. What do I need to do?"

"You need to give me an updated resume. I will forward it to him and connect you."

I did as she asked, and about two weeks later, I had an appointment with Sam.

He wanted to meet in a café in the historic Healey Building's lobby in downtown Atlanta. That wasn't my first time in downtown Atlanta. Some college friends and I went to Underground Atlanta with some frat boys from Georgia Tech to a place called Fat Tuesdays for someone's 21st birthday. It was the 1990s in Atlanta, and downtown and Underground was getting a big refurbish in preparation for The Olympics.

But I had not been to downtown in the daytime, during business hours. The people on the street were office workers. The other people on the street were living there. Still do, sadly.

Sam gave me instructions to park in a lot on Ellis Street, behind the Peachtree Center MARTA station and across the street from The Ritz Carlton. It was a Parking Company of America lot.

From there, I walked up the hill on Ellis Street toward Peachtree Street, turned left and headed toward historic Five Points, the center of Atlanta. Five Points is where five main railroad lines connected and established an area called "Terminus" before the name was changed to Atlanta.

I remember trying not to get blown away by the wind tunnel in front of the Georgia-Pacific Building, the original site of the Loew's Grand Theater, where "Gone with the Wind" premiered in 1939. It's coincidental that one of the windiest parts of Atlanta is where "Gone with the Wind" premiered. The struggle not to get blown away by the wind tunnel in downtown would become a daily struggle for the next eighteen years of my life.

With the printed Mapquest directions in hand, I found the Healey Building and went in at the Broad Street entrance.

The antique wood revolving doors took me inside of the building. It was breathtaking. I didn't know such beautiful architecture existed in Atlanta. The light, the marble floors, and the brass elevators spoke history and fortitude. There was a barber shop in the lobby, a family-owned jewelry store, and a café.

Sam was seated at a table for two in the lobby café. I felt like I was in France and not in Atlanta. He wore a bowtie and had a full head of curly dark hair. He stood up as I walked toward him, and held his hand out and said, "I'm Sam Zama-rri-pa," annunciating the last name. A last name I would spend the next ten years spelling for everyone.

We talked for almost four hours, and I'm not sure it was even a job interview anymore. I found my long lost uncle. I was moving forward to find a career and a family in Atlanta, and I found it in the Hispanic community.

Sam opened a Public Affairs firm on the fourth floor of the Flatiron building in downtown Atlanta. There was no furniture in our three-room office suite yet. I sat on the floor and had my laptop on a chair, a Macbook from 1995. I still have that laptop in my garage. It means more to me than some of my family photos.

I did everything. I answered the phone, typed letters, and paid the bills. One time I forgot to pay the phone bill. That was a very bad day. I was "His Girl, Friday."

Then one day, Sam excitedly said to me, "Maria! We have new clients! They're Spaniards, and they're coming to

Atlanta for the Olympics." He said we were going to help them promote tourism to Spain and increase sales of Jamon Serrano. He wanted to partner with everybody, including Diaz Foods. The Spaniards were going to build a Spanish pavilion in downtown Atlanta on the parking lot where I parked, so Sam said we would have to find me another parking spot. He continued to prepare me with, "You'll be translating a lot and helping me manage their lead, Carmen. Also, get some ashtrays for the office. Spaniards smoke."

The next day, I quit my second job at Victoria's Secret in Underground Atlanta. I worked long hours. I chauffeured Carmen around, went to many events, met many Spaniards, ate well, drank good Spanish wine, went to the Olympics, dusted cigarette ash off the desks, and had a complete blast. I've never gone to Spain, probably because I felt like Spain came to me.

In 1998, Sam said to me, "Maria! I've taken the SVP of Public Affairs job at the Metro Atlanta Chamber of Commerce, and I'm going to work for Sam Williams. I'm closing the office down, but I got you a job at Ketchum Public Relations in midtown in the 999 Peachtree Building. The managing director is Jane Shivers. You're going to work for the Community Relations Practice and report to Jan Pomerantz. You'll be an assistant account executive, low on the totem pole, but you will learn communications."

We packed up the office. On my last day, Sam took me to lunch and gave me a book about "Shamans." Shamans are people of wisdom, healing, and are believed to be able to commune with spirits and act as intermediaries between good and evil.

He told me, "Maria, look for the Shamans in this new workplace. Also, you are there to make everyone above you look good. Never forget that." I never forgot that.

I went to Ketchum, my first corporate job ever. I was scared to death and wanted to fit in. I learned how to write press releases. I pitched media over the phone in the pitch booth. I worked on promoting the corporate foundations of clients like Delta Air Lines and Georgia Power. I had to work hard and stay within a budgeted amount of billable hours.

Eleven months later, Sam called me with a smile in his voice and announced, "Maria! I have an opportunity for you. We need an executive director for the Arts & Business Council for the Metro Atlanta Chamber. You like the arts, right?" He explained that the role would be connecting businesses to the arts. He said I would need to learn how to fundraise and manage a board. He told me I would still need to submit a resume and interview for the job.

That was my first executive director job. But two weeks before I started the job, Sam walked me down the aisle to marry Tony.

Back to downtown Atlanta I went. The Chamber building was on Centennial Olympic Park. And once again, I struggled every day not to get blown away by the wind tunnel as I walked across the park to work. I had an office that overlooked International Blvd. It wasn't a big office, but just the right size. At this point, the number of people I was meeting and my exposure to leaders in the region felt like a tsunami. I could tell some people felt I got that job because I had a champion, rather than qualifications. They weren't wrong. I learned to fail, and fail fast, so I could get back up, learn from the mistake and do better. I learned to work with difficult personalities. But still, I was having a ball.

Somewhere in there, 9/11 happened, and like all Americans, we had heavy hearts in Atlanta. At the time, I lived in a loft downtown on Marietta Street, and the west view of the loft looked right at CNN. It was a weird sensation to watch CNN report on this tragedy, knowing it was just 6 blocks from me. 9/11 didn't feel far away. It felt very close.

In 2002, Sam called me again and jovially said, "Maria! I'm running for State Senate District 36. I could be one of the first Hispanics in the State Legislature. Come work on my campaign! You'll learn how political campaigns and government work." The campaign office was going to be in Midtown on the corner of West Peachtree and 14th Street across from the IBM Building, in a building that would later be torn down and redeveloped. 20,000 cars went by that location each day at that time. Only 20,000 cars. Those were the good old days.

Back to midtown I went again. During the campaign, we went into communities in the district. People hosted campaign events in their homes—Inman Park, Midtown, Druid Hills, parts of Morningside. I learned how to fundraise from individuals. I met more people. I learned how to listen to people's needs. I was still having the time of my life.

Halfway through the campaign, we were in the office one afternoon. The office was a retail space with a wall of windows and a loft on the second floor. It was open throughout, and no one had walls. My desk was between the window and the water cooler.

As had become typical fashion, Sam said, "Maria! I'm going to forward an email to you. Take the job."

"What job?"

"Just check your email."

It turns out that ING moved its Americas Headquarters to Atlanta, and they were moving the ING Foundation here. The new president of the foundation was not originally from Atlanta, and she was looking for a Community Relations Manager who understood the Atlanta community and understood philanthropy. I had never been through a job interview like that before. They flew me to Hartford, Connecticut to meet with the group president, who was a *woman*. She was managing millions. As I look back on that time, there were many women at the top of that organization, and they were diverse women. All of my bosses were women there, except for a very brief moment when our department was in transition and we reported to the General Counsel, who was a man.

This was my second corporate job, and I worked for ING for six years. The headquarters was on Powers Ferry Road, the offices were referred to as "the campus." It had a long, gently curved driveway with a tree canopy that was just breathtaking in the spring and fall. There was a walking and running trail and a bird sanctuary behind the building. There were two buildings, the main headquarters and the other called "The Pavilion." It had a cafeteria, work out room, and basketball gym for employees.

The foundation had a giving budget of $5.8 million per year, an employee volunteerism program, employee giving campaign, and a diversity and inclusion program. I traveled about a third of the time, helping executives represent the company in communities where we had major offices. That included New York City, Twin Cities, Los Angeles, Scottsdale, Miami, and others. The foundation's platform was financial literacy, so we sponsored Junior Achievement in various communities. But we supported other causes, too, like the arts, United Way, and Earth Share.

I worked for the company when they purchased the sponsorship rights for the New York City Marathon, and it was called "The ING New York City Marathon." They sponsored marathons all over the country, and I mostly worked on the "Run for Something Better" community outreach program. Now I was meeting people nationally and learning about communities outside Atlanta. I was helping employees in various offices find volunteer opportunities.

Later, I would reflect on how magical that job was. Community relations jobs don't just come along like that. And the people I worked with there were tremendous. I hope some of them will read these words and know how grateful I was for that experience.

Needless to say, my mother loved Sam. He made her laugh. But mostly because she knew someone was looking after me. She called him before she called me to tell him about my adoption. She said to him, "She's going to need you after I tell her." And she was right. I called Sam after she told me. He said to me, "A little bit of sadness in life is good." Well, I have had my fair share of sadness.

Mom would give Sam and his family boxes of mangoes. I think this is why they named a family dog "Mango." Poor Mango smelled so bad. She met her demise on a dirt road by a truck near their river house in Ellijay, Georgia.

Mom would also make Sam and his family "pandesal," a Filipino sweet bread that took hours to make. If Mom cooked for you, she liked you. If Mom made you pandesal, she loved you.

I have learned many things from Sam, but mostly how to explore things, to re-invent myself, and adapt to change. If it weren't for these lessons, I don't know how I would've had the courage to start my own consulting business in community affairs in 2009, at the height of the recession. After the ING job, I learned to take the wheel of my own trajectory, which included a two-year community relations stint at Troutman Sanders until the recession hit. When the economy fell apart in 2009, Tony and I had a new baby. It was a scary time. When I started consulting, I was finding nonprofit and for-profit clients who needed help, but couldn't make a full time hire. I would work projects for them. I had thirteen clients by the time I shuttered my firm to take the job at Leadership DeKalb. The recession was difficult, and my consulting business allowed me to pay my basic bills, but debt was looming, and our real estate value had tanked. I am deeply grateful to the people in my network who gave me projects during that difficult time.

Sam is always just a call away when I need a Shaman. He's written books, married off two daughters, and continues to be innovative and thoughtful about the world.

Because of Sam, I look for Shamans in all the places. Little did I know that in 2013, I would find myself in a leadership nonprofit where all the Shamans congregate.

Me and Sam on Thanksgiving 2017.

CHAPTER 9

Christopher Jay

Tony and I had been together for ten years, and we were sure we were never going to have children. We were so sure about this that we chose a lifestyle that didn't accommodate children. We lived in a high-rise loft in downtown Atlanta, with no parking attached to the building. We moved into that building in 1996, right after the Olympics. I converted one of the bedrooms into my closet, and we were out every night with friends, drinking martinis or wine at a rooftop patio or one of the local restaurants. We were the quintessential "DINKS"— double income, no kids.

We lived at The Metropolitan on Marietta Street in downtown, and the building was originally an Art Deco building, built around the same time as The William-Oliver and The Healey Building. But city leaders decided in the 1970s, they needed to have a "Wall Street" center of commerce part of town, and they converted Marietta Street into a mini-Wall Street and set out to modernize the historical buildings. As a result, developers covered the old Art Deco buildings with fiberglass facades, creating a contemporary, hard edged feel for the street that historically connected to Five Points in downtown Atlanta.

The *Atlanta Journal-Constitution*, the Atlanta newspaper, was located on Marietta Street and about three blocks from our condo. CNN Center was just two more blocks beyond that. Our condo was actually two units connected. We had the A unit and B unit, and the two units were connected by ten-foot glass French doors. The Metropolitan had seventeen and a half floors in the main building, and then there was a half building adjacent to the main building. Tony and I had lived in four separate apartments in that building. At the beginning in 1996, he lived on the eighteenth floor, a half floor unit and the "penthouse," and I lived in a seventeenth-floor efficiency, which was basically my closet. I did this as a technicality. My mother was going to disown me if I lived with a man unmarried. Well, technically, I did not live with Tony. I was his neighbor.

Tony and I were living a wonderful city life. We were gainfully employed, and I was jetting all over the country doing meaningful, yet fun, work. Tony jetted around too. He was working for a company called "Play." They were a strategic planning company that utilized cartoon artists to help illustrate outcomes of strategic planning sessions. Tony *loved* working for Play! He was especially good at it because of his caricature art training. But he also had a special talent for listening to people's ideas and illustrating those ideas on a giant cartoon. Remarkable talent. He was having a blast.

It was October 2006, when Tony was on one of these trips for Play in Florida. I was at home in Atlanta and had had a nagging feeling tugging at me for a week. My period was really late. On my way home from work, I decided to stop at CVS and pick up a pregnancy test. I recall picking out the kind where the color would change if you were pregnant.

So, I was home alone because Tony was on the road. I peed on the stick. I had to wait two minutes. By the way, for those of you who have never "peed on a stick," this waiting period (pun totally intended) for the pregnancy result, is *the* longest wait of your life. Whether you think it will be "good news" or "bad news," the wait is eternal.

I stood there in the bathroom, staring at the pregnancy test. Then ever so slowly, it started to change color. The color got more pronounced. And then I said to myself, "No fucking way. No fucking way!"

I went to my bedroom, grabbed my purse, and threw on my shoes. I remember pushing and pushing the elevator button in the hall, anxious to get out of the condo building so I could drive to either Publix or CVS to get more pregnancy tests. I do not recall which store it was where I ended up. I got different kinds of tests: the color changing kind, the kind that says "Pregnant" or "Not Pregnant." I got the kind that had a "+" or "-"sign. I got different brands.

I guzzled a tall glass of water to get fluids in my system so I could take more tests.

I do not recall how many there were in total, but I had them all lined up on the bathroom counter, and every single one of them said, "Maria, you are pregnant."

Shit.

I dialed Tony but got no answer. I waited fifteen minutes, but still no answer. I called him every fifteen minutes for an hour and half. Finally, he called back. He said, "What the hell? I have like ten missed calls from you."

"You need to sit down."

"What? Why? I can't sit down. I'm in a big lobby of a conference center, and we just got out of a banquet dinner. That's why my phone was off. What is it? Just tell me."

"No, dude, you need to sit down."

"Okay. Let me find a corner, and I'll just sit down." He disappeared from the line for a moment. There were shuffling noises in the background before he spoke again. "Okay, I'm sitting. What's up?!"

"I'm pregnant."

Silence. Then he exclaimed, "What?!"

"I'm pregnant."

He chuckled, and I could hear him push air out of the corner of his mouth, "No, you're not."

"Yes, I am."

"No, you're not."

"Yes, I am. I've taken about half a dozen pregnancy tests, and I'm pregnant."

"No, you're not."

"Yes, I am."

"NO. YOU'RE NOT."

"YES, I AM!!"

"Oh, shit."

"Oh, shit is right."

The next day, Tony made the long drive back to Atlanta, and I went to work like a regular day. I knew I wouldn't see him until I got home from work that evening. I was distracted all day. I couldn't focus on emails or any documents. I was anxious to get home and talk to Tony. But I also didn't want to leave work early, because then I would just be at home, pacing the floor. I was actually grateful for the distraction of being at the office, and I used that time to think. I was meditative and giving myself the day to adjust and get used to the idea that I was going to be a mother.

When I got home that evening, he was already there.

He said, "Okay. What's this pregnancy business?"

I said, "Hold on." I went straight to my bathroom and gathered all the pregnancy tests. I brought them to the dining room. "Look."

He looked carefully and realized all of them were positive.

"Well, what the hell are we going to do?! We're not ready to be parents!"

"What do you mean, 'What are we going to do?' We are going to be parents. That's all there is to it."

"Where are we going to put this baby? Where are you going to put all your shoes?"

This may seem like a funny question, but it was actually a very valid point. Where was I going to put all my shoes? And handbags? Where were we going to put this baby? And this wasn't just a literal question, it was a metaphorical one, too. We were living a lifestyle that wasn't suited for a child. I loved my career and all the travel, and Tony was a full-time artist who kept weird hours. We were not suited to be parents. We felt like kids ourselves.

We were both trying to wrap our heads around the idea of being parents. We were both on edge and it was a very difficult time.

But I was getting used to the idea of a baby growing inside of me. I told my mother I was pregnant, and she said, "Good. It will give your life more meaning. God wants to know just how much you can love."

Her words rang through to the deepest part of my soul. I thought I already knew love. I thought I understood love, but obviously, I did not.

Toward the end of my first trimester, I lost that baby. Just as I did not know true love, I did not know true depression. I crashed and burned in unexpected ways. I was heartbroken and just broken. I had already been thinking about names for this new person. I would run my hands through the baby clothes hanging at Target and wish for a little girl I could dress in sparkly tutus, patent leather Mary Janes, and little pink tights. I could already feel the changes in my body. My rib cage was getting wider, and my slender waist started to disappear. But

I lost that baby, and I mourn that baby every day. How can I mourn someone so deeply whom I have never met?

The national debate about when a human life actually begins hit me right in my heart. I believe in a woman's right to choose. I always have, and I always will, but how I feel about the little embryo in my belly? That right there is complicated. I cannot explain how I began to love that unborn baby so much. I cannot explain it. I just did. Maybe it was the hormones. Maybe it was my mother's words influencing my thoughts and feelings. I don't know. I just loved…love…that unborn baby.

I lost that baby close to the holidays, and a very small group of close friends knew about it. One of them gave me a Christmas ornament. It's a hand painted eggshell from her trip to Prague. The paint is this vibrant navy blue, and it's a delicate and graceful scroll pattern all around the egg. It has a blue satin ribbon from which you can hang the ornament on the tree. When she gave it to me, she said, "This is for the baby."

That ornament has a its own compartment in a special ornament storage box. When I put up my Christmas tree, I place that ornament in the center of the tree toward the top, and I always make sure it's near one of the little bulbs of the tree lights so it is illuminated. And when I hang that ornament, I am gentle and careful to place it on a pine needle that is pointed upward so it doesn't slide off. And then I say to myself, "I love you, little baby. Rest in peace."

After the loss of that baby, the depression was excruciating. But there was something else, too. Through that pregnancy, God showed me an alternate reality for my future. It was as if God said, "You have seen what's behind door number one and door number two. Now let Me show you what's behind door number three." The scenes I pictured were holidays, birthday parties, sports activities, laughing, and giggling. And I also pictured another human being that could look like me. I began to recall the feeling of meeting that one distant cousin in Manila who was blood related to me. I recalled the feeling of belonging when I saw someone with my same features. As an adopted person, I could not go backwards in my blood line, so why couldn't I go forwards? This applied to my legacy and also wanting to be a mother. Living my old lifestyle was now out of the question. I wanted to be a mother, and I wanted it deeply and immensely. If ovaries could ache, then my ovaries ached. My womb wanted to breed life. By the following February, I was pregnant again.

My due date was November 15, 2008. We got a contractor to renovate the loft to accommodate my closet and a baby. You know that notion about pregnant women who nest? Well, my nesting was about $25,000. Every waking moment I was looking at paint swatches and ordering tile samples. The contractor built a new closet in the main bedroom, he renovated the master suite bathroom completely, and he included a spacious counter for the baby's changing table. My closet had sliding doors. One section was shelves just for the shoes! He put in all new carpet in the master suite and the nursery. My friend Claire, who is an Agnes Scott classmate and professional designer, helped me design the nursery. I hired a textile decorator named Andre who sewed all the drapes and pillows for the nursery. The condo was chaos, and we had to live in the space while all the renovations were being done.

But even in the midst of all this chaos, I got up every day and went to work. I was at Troutman Sanders Law Firm during this time, working as the Community Relations Manager. The office was in the Bank of America tower in Midtown Atlanta. My office was on the forty-sixth floor, and my parking spot was in a lot located across the street on North Avenue.

One day, Bob the office administrator said to me, "Maria,

I'm going to get you a parking space in the garage in the building."

I was surprised. "Really? I have a spot across the street, though."

He said, "I know, but...well, you're very pregnant, and I just don't feel comfortable with you walking half a block and crossing that busy intersection." It was West Peachtree and North Avenue, and he wasn't wrong.

Bob was a Former Marine and a perfect gentleman. He went on to work for the Centers for Disease Control for a while, and we stayed in touch over the years after that. I will never forget his kind gesture. I graciously accepted his offer, because I was actually waddling. I gained forty-two pounds during my pregnancy, and I swear about twenty pounds of it were my boobs.

You know that character Violet Beauregard from "Charlie and the Chocolate Factory?" Violet, against Mr. Willy Wonka's advice, chewed some experimental bubble gum which caused her to turn into a giant blueberry. She grew rounder and rounder and inflated until she was a blueberry with little arms and legs sticking out. That was me. Round with little arms and legs sticking out.

I will say this, though. Even during my pregnancy, I did not give up on fashion. I refused to give up my favorite shoes. I shoved my swelling feet and ankles into high heels and boots. I was going to be damned if I didn't look cute, fashionable, and pregnant at the same time.

It was exactly this issue that got me in "good trouble," as Congressman John Lewis would say. It was October 29, 2008, about two weeks from my due date. It was a beautiful, sunny fall day in Atlanta. While getting ready for work, I felt it was a good day to wear my black and brown fall maternity dress with brown leather boots. But there was one problem. My pregnant belly was so huge, I could not bend over to zip up my boots. I told myself, *Maria, don't give up. If you can't bend forward to zip these boots up, then bend backwards and zip them up. You were a dancer, you can do this.*

I looped a belt around foot of the bed, creating a strap. I looped the other end of that strap to my right wrist, and using the bed's weight as a counter-balance, I bent backwards to zip up one boot. Then I switched hands and zipped up the other boot. Mission accomplished!

When I straightened up and looked at myself in the mirror, I felt good about how I had won my fashion war against pregnancy. But then I felt a tightening on the left side of my belly.

I rubbed it with my left hand and thought it was just tight muscles from my current condition.

I left the condo for work and walked down the hall to the elevator. When I reached the elevator, I felt the tightening in my belly again. This time, I felt it on both sides.

By the time I got down to the lobby of my building, I had decided to call my OBGYN's office.

I dialed and told the receptionist, "Hi, this is Maria Balais. I'm a patient of Dr. Williams. Is she available, or can I talk to one of her nurses?"

"Ms. Balais, Dr. Williams is off today. Dr. Hood is the doctor on call today. Would you like to speak to her P.A.?"

"Yes, that would be fine."

A nurse came on the line and asked, "Ms. Balais, how are you feeling today?"

"I'm fine, but I'm feeling this tightening in my belly, and I think I should come in this afternoon. Can you fit me in?"

"Let me look at your chart." I hear the clicking of a keyboard in the background. "It looks like you are due in a couple of weeks. Yes, I think you should come in immediately."

"Well, I'd rather come after lunch. I have a 10:30 a.m. meeting and then I have a lunch meeting. I can be there by 1:30 p.m."

"But Ms. Balais, I really think you need to come on in."

"Nah, I'm fine. Can't I call you mid-morning and give you an update? I'm not due for another two weeks. This is probably indigestion."

I am the worst patient on the planet. I know more than doctors and nurses.

"But the due date is a window, and you could be in labor."

"Labor! I'm not in labor! I'm not in any pain. I'm just uncomfortable because I had to zip up some boots."

"Boots? What about boots? I'm not sure what you're talking about, Ms. Balais, but I think you need to come in."

"Okay. I'll come in. I'll see you at 1:30 p.m. Thank you!" And before she could protest, I hung up.

I drove to the office, and it wasn't long after I arrived that someone noticed what was happening to me. Dorothy, an older black woman who oversaw the pro-bono work for the firm, stared intently at me down the hall. Then she loudly proclaimed, "Maria, honey, you've dropped!"

I said, "What? What are you talking about, Dorothy?"

She walked closer and answered, "Honey, I'm telling you, you've dropped. You're fixing to have that baby."

"Nah. I'm not due for another two weeks."

"Uh, huh. Okay, baby. But I'm telling you, you've dropped."

With that, she shook her head, walked back to her office and closed the door. I shrugged it off.

So I went to my 10:30 meeting, then I went to my lunch meeting with my work colleagues. One co-worker affirmed my fashion choices with, "Oh, those are really cute boots!"

I agreed, "Yes! I love these boots. They're the perfect chocolate brown."

At 1:00 p.m., I returned to my office and started organizing my desk. Then I let my colleagues know I was leaving early to go to the doctor. Everyone was in enthusiastic agreement.

"Yes! Great idea, Maria! Go to the doctor!" I thought it was odd that they were all so eager for me to go.

I took the long elevator ride down to the main lobby of the office tower. My ears popped in the elevator, as the forty-sixth floor is pretty high up. I took a second set of elevators to the parking garage. At that point, I had to squeeze myself behind the steering wheel. I made the drive to Buckhead to the medical building behind Piedmont Hospital. I went into my OBGYN's office, the receptionist recognized me. She waved me back, "Ms. Balais! Come straight back, right now, please!"

They immediately put me in an exam room. A technician taped wires on my belly so that a machine could track my contractions.

About twenty minutes later, Dr. Hood came in and said, "Hello, Maria. How are you?"

"I'm great! How are you?"

"We're having a good day here. Good to hear you're fine. Are you in any pain?"

"Nope."

"Okay. Well, let's see what we have here." She hit a button that printed out a long sheet of paper like ticker tape. It showed a continuous line that made peaks and valleys. Dr. Hood just said, "Hmm."

"So what does that say?" I asked.

"I'm going to send you to L&D."

"L&D? What's that?"

"Labor and delivery."

"What?!"

She enunciated slowly, "Lay-bor and deli-ve-ry."

"I'm having this baby?"

"Yes, you are, in fact, having a baby."

"Wait a minute. I'm not due for another two weeks."

"Well, he's ready to come now."

"But I'm not in any pain."

"You're going to be in pain. A lot of pain. You are scheduled for a C-section, so we can do surgery prep at 3:00 p.m., and you can have this baby by 5:00 p.m. today."

"But, I'm not ready! I haven't finished putting together the nursery! He can't come early!"

"He's ready to come out. I'm sending you to L&D."

"Okay, Dr. Hood, look. I realize I sound crazy. In fact, I feel crazy. I have been thinking about becoming a mother. I have thoroughly enjoyed being pregnant. It's been a great pregnancy, but I didn't think about the actual part where I have the baby. Can I have a couple of hours to adjust to this?"

"Ms. Balais, you've had nine months to adjust to having a baby."

"I know. But I need just two more hours."

She squinted at me and pursed her lips tightly. She mulled over her authority as my doctor. Finally she said, "Okay. The last surgery slot for the day is at 8:00 p.m. You have to report to L&D at exactly 6:00 p.m. for prep. Otherwise, you will push this baby out."

"Okay, deal!"

I rushed out of the doctor's office and called Tony, who was at a caricature job.

"Hello?"

"He's coming! The baby is coming! I'm in labor!"

"What?! You're not due for another two weeks!"

"Apparently, the due date is an estimation."

Poor Tony. He was just getting dragged into fatherhood. He had no control of anything whatsoever. "Well, do I need to meet you at the hospital?"

"No, meet me at home. I need to put together a suitcase, and I want to finish the nursery."

"What? Are you kidding me? You want to finish decorating the nursery?"

"It's already decorated. I just need to do some finishing touches. I can't have this baby until that nursery is done."

How could I possibly explain to Tony that it wasn't about the nursery and that it was about how I needed a couple of hours to become a mother?

Back in downtown Atlanta, I parked my car in the valet parking across the street from our condo building on the corner of Marietta Street and Broad Street, at the old Commerce Club building. I crossed that busy intersection with my handbag in the crook of my right arm and my left hand cradling the underside of my big belly, as if I could prevent that baby from falling out in the middle of the street. I waddled into the building and up to the condo. When I walked in the door, Tony was already there.

We got the nursery put together, I packed a suitcase, and we left around 4:45 p.m. to beat rush hour traffic. We took Peachtree Street all the way up north from downtown to Buckhead.

When we arrived at the L&D floor of the hospital, there was a bell on the counter of the nurse's station like the ones that used to be on the check-in desk of old hotels. You tapped on the top of it and it went "Ding!" I felt like I was checking into a hotel rather than going into surgery and coming out with a baby.

The surgery prep went quickly. I was more afraid of the epidural than anything. The idea that someone was about to stick a long giant needle into my spinal cord just freaked me out.

The sensation of the C-section was also weird. Dr. Hood

said things like, "Okay, I'm gonna move some of your organs around, and you're going to feel some pressure."

Holy crap. She was moving my organs around.

Then she said to Tony, who was standing by my head, "Dad, would you like to come see? Do you want to cut the cord?"

Tony says, "No thanks. I'm good. You go right ahead."

I don't blame Tony one bit. I felt that was the correct response.

Then, after a few minutes, I hear it. "Wah! Wah! Wah!"

Tony says, "Oh my God! There he is, and he looks so gross. So gross!"

"Don't worry, Dad. We'll clean him up and give him right back to you."

The rest was a blur. I was on some great drugs. The next two weeks were also a blur. I've had insomnia many times, and I knew what it felt like to have a sleepless night. But those early weeks were not "sleepless nights." They were sleep deprivation, the kind of sleep deprivation used in torture.

We named the baby Christopher Jay, after Tony's two lifelong best friends, Christopher and DeeJay. Tony considers them his brothers, and so do I. It was my idea to name him after the brothers, and it was also my idea to nickname him "CJ."

One week after we brought CJ home, Barack Obama was elected President. Living in downtown Atlanta, election night seemed more like New Year's Eve. There was honking and loud music coming from cars in celebration all night, and some firecrackers. We could hear people rejoicing outside, "Woo-hoo! A black man is President! Yeah, that's right!"

CJ's birth was one of the happiest days of my life. I know it was for Tony, too. Neither Tony nor I knew how to really love before CJ was born. And then for his birth to be timed with the election of the first black President was icing on the cake.

One last thing. As I write this, the date is October 29, 2019. CJ turned 11 today. I didn't plan to write this chapter tonight, but here I am. Everything about my life has been good fortune, even the sad moments, and it doesn't surprise me one bit that the timing of writing this chapter is exactly what it is. By now, my faith in God and the Universe is as solid as a rock.

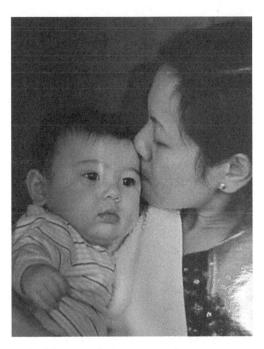

Me holding my baby, CJ, at The Zamarripa's river house in Ellijay, GA, 2009.

PART 3

Everyone Else

CHAPTER 10

The Crazed Asian Woman

I cannot write chapters about everyone else without writing one about myself. I am the Crazed Asian Woman. It is obvious by now that I have had some very serious and sad chapters in my life, but it is not just full of tragedy. There is also lots of comedy.

The self-deprecating variety is one of my favorite kinds of humor, and with me, there is plenty of material. Because life doesn't happen *to* me; it happens *at* me. I constantly feel like I am being secretly filmed and punk'd. Or maybe it's just my choice to see the humor in life.

Let's begin with how tiny I am. I am blessed to be proportionate, but I am *tiny*. I'm 4' 9" tall, and I weigh 90 pounds. I stopped growing in the 7th grade. When I have to speak at a podium, I bring a folding step stool. I just pop that sucker open behind the podium, and I hop right on it. Although, lately, I've been requesting a lavalier mic whenever possible and avoid the podium altogether, because I think I might be shrinking with age. That really happens, you know.

I have to buy underwear in the girls' section at Target because the women's XS underwear is still too big. When I sleep at night and turn over in bed, the big underwear twists around, and it's very uncomfortable. I told a friend this once and she said, "What, do you have princesses on your undies?"

"No! Unicorns."

She guffawed on that one.

Also, I hate baths. While baths are soothing and comfortable for most people, to me they are treacherous. I cannot reach the other end of the tub to anchor myself, and basically, I float in the tub and feel like I'm drowning. I hate baths. Besides, why would I want to soak in my own dirt?

Being trapped in a small Asian body is just half the battle. There are external forces too. For example, leaf blowers and down pours. For some inexplicable reason, whenever I have to be dressed up, like for a gala or an important meeting, there are four leaf blowers outside my apartment or my office, or there will be a heavy downpour. I'm punk'd by the Universe, I tell ya.

On one occasion, I had an 8:30 a.m. meeting. I was going to meet a board to secure our funding for our organization. I had on my favorite gray H&M sheath dress and navy-blue Jessica Simpson pumps, which are very high heels in the first place. I walked out of my office building in downtown Decatur to walk to the Task Force for Global Health building on Swanton Way for the meeting. This is about a five-block walk. Right outside the building were two leaf blowers, and the guys wielding them had on noise canceling headphones, so they couldn't hear me or see me. I flapped my right arm as hard as I could to get their attention, to no avail. I gave up and skirted around them to get to the sidewalk. My eyes started itching from all the dust, at which point the bottled water nestled in my purse fell out and started rolling down the hill of the parking lot toward the street. I scurried in my sheath dress and high heels, trying to catch the bottled water...click-click-click-click in my high heel shoes, when a bulb went on in my head, *Screw it! Get to the meeting! They will have water at the meeting!*

It was late May, and the weather was warm. When I got to the meeting, I was out of breath, thirsty as hell, and perspiring. I was so worried my deodorant wore off that I kept my upper arms down as I shook hands with people. I have carried deodorant in my purse since that incident.

But the downpours are really when I feel punk'd. One time I went to a book signing at the Dunwoody Nature Center, and the clouds were deep gray and ominous all day. The sky looked like it was going to crack open any minute, but it wouldn't rain. In the car on my way to my next event, my driver says, "It's going to rain. You have on those nice shoes."

"I know. Please hurry and get me to Midtown."

"I have to get you there safely. So you might have to get soaked."

It started sprinkling, but the sky didn't open up until the moment I was being dropped off at the sidewalk and getting out of the car. I got soaked. It took three days for my shoes to dry out. This happened to me on at least two other occasions.

But the best times are when I walk into a spiderweb, which happens to me often, because there is a tree canopy over the staircase of my townhouse apartment. The spiders weave webs between the rails of the staircase which I have to navigate to get to my driveway. When I walk into a web, my knee jerk reaction is to propel my handbag like a helicopter, looking like a Samurai ninja on meth. This is why I carry handbags with zippers, so all my stuff doesn't fall out.

Spiderwebs happen at least once a month. But losing my car in the parking garage at work happens every day. Every. Single. Day. And it's not like the parking garage is huge. It's only a four-story parking garage in downtown Decatur. But the floors all look alike, and one day blends into the next. I've tried all kinds of tricks, like taking a photo with my phone, but then I have a gallery of photos of the parking garage in my phone. Who wants that? I tried the parking app, but the stupid app doesn't work, because there's terrible signal in the garage. I also learned that for some odd reason, when I get to the entrance of the garage, I have to pee! It's like a Pavlovian reaction. Probably because I'm anxious about looking for my car. The most stressful days are when I have a meeting in the middle of the day and I have to move my car. On days like that, I just take slow, deep breaths. So I've embraced the situation and thank the heavens I have a place to park for free in downtown Decatur. Now, I just budget an extra fifteen minutes to get out of the garage...five minutes to pee first...ten minutes to walk from the bottom floor until I find my car. I get my exercise.

And I need the exercise, because I started menopause. Why does society feel uncomfortable talking about menopause? In fact, the word "menopause" is euphemistically referred to as "The Change." Get over it, people. This is a natural part of a woman's life, and we are too hot and cranky to skirt the issue. And there is a distinction between perimenopause and menopause, which I think is just ridiculous, because the symptoms are the same. My main symptom are migraine headaches, and those started in April of 2017. If you think migraines are just headaches, you are so wrong. But I didn't fully grasp that I had started menopause until early in summer of 2019. Here's what happened. A bird had nested in a tree outside my bedroom window. The eggs hatched, and the chicks tweeted all the time. They irritated me so much that one night, I found myself Googling semi-automatic BB guns. That's when I knew my mood swing had gone to another level.

One night, I overheard my son, who is now 11, talking on his headset to a friend, "My mom is in a really bad mood.

Something about 'minion paws.' I'm really confused because minions don't have paws."

Well, I embrace minion paws. I have a minion paws fan on my desk, which can be turned around to the guest chair for my lovely friends who also have minion paws. I carry a lovely fan in my purse, which is now a staple part of my wardrobe and the act of fanning myself an affectation. I also carry a pashmina or cardigan sweater, because with minion paws, you can be having a hot flash one minute and then freezing cold the next. I moisturize. I watch my diet. And most importantly, I count to ten and watch my smart mouth. That last one is the hardest.

Watching my smart mouth is not as hard as fixing my face, though. My professional female friends are great friends, because when we are in meetings, and it gets intense, one of them will text me: "Gurrl, fix yo face." The funny text eases me and I take a deep breath and relax my face and concentrate on lifting up the corners of my mouth for a slight smile. But you also have to let your eyes smile, otherwise, you look like you just had Botox done.

Little inconveniences in life happen all the time, but I just roll with it and try to see the humor in everything. Many of the pages in this next section are really about that. I love entertainment, and there is plenty of live entertainment all around me in real life.

CHAPTER 11

The People at the Supermarket

I have to be in the right frame of mind to go grocery shopping, and not because I am anxious about what to buy or anything like that, but because of the people I encounter at the supermarket. Everyone has to go grocery shopping at some point—*everyone*. So the supermarket is a microcosm of America.

I frequent two supermarkets, and both are Publix. One Publix is located on Ponce de Leon Avenue in Midtown, but adjacent to the Poncey Highlands and Inman Park neighborhoods. This Publix is located between my office in Decatur and my house downtown. It's very convenient when I want to grocery shop on the way home from work. The parking for this one is a surface lot with one side facing Ponce and the other side facing North Highland Avenue. Because it is in a more residential part of town, there are more families who shop at this Publix. We'll call this Publix the Ponce Publix.

The other Publix is located in Midtown in the retail space

of a residential high rise called Midtown Plaza. This is also the supermarket for most of the Georgia Tech students and has a very international graduate school clientele. The parking for this one is a covered parking garage, which is very convenient when it's a rainy day, because there is nothing worse in my opinion than trying to load groceries into your car in the rain. We'll call this one the Midtown Publix.

When CJ was a toddler, I took him grocery shopping with me one afternoon at the Midtown Publix and I decided it would be fun to use one of the grocery carts which looks like a big toy car. CJ was really into cars and trains at that age and he was thrilled to sit inside a big toy car. I used one of those baby grocery cart blanket liners—the kind they now make for mothers who are afraid of germs touching their babies. I was one of those mothers. It was soft cotton with blue stripes on the inside and light blue with a washable and durable outer lining on the outside. It had pockets on the edge where you could put stuffy toys. It was a tricked-out grocery liner.

I popped the baby on my hip and placed the diaper bag underneath the cart. Then I got the liner situated with one hand. This took a few minutes, and I realized people were going around me to get a cart out of the corral. I ignored them. Then I got my baby inside the cart and put his little fat legs through the leg holes of the baby car seat.

I grabbed ahold of the handle and began to pull the cart out of the corral. Only then did I realize how heavy the cart was. As a reminder, I am 4' 9" tall and weigh about 90 pounds. I quickly realized the cart was too heavy for me. I decided to abort the idea of the toy car cart, and I started to get CJ out and into a regular cart. But NOPE. He would not have any of that. He started to cry.

"Wah! Wah! No! No!"

"Baby, Mommy can't push the cart, Shh-shh-shh. We will use the cart next time when Daddy is with us."

I was a new mother, and I stupidly thought I could reason with a toddler.

"*Wah! Wah!* No! No! Car! Car!"

The entrance to this store is adjacent to the concrete parking garage. Have you ever noticed the echoes in parking garages? That's because of the solid, hard concrete surface, and there is nothing to absorb sound. So a toddler screaming at the top of his lungs in a parking garage is a mother's worst nightmare.

At this point, people started staring. I could feel the judgmental stares of young, hipster, single people who mostly shopped at this store. "Get your baby under control, lady. Do we have to call DFCS?"

I used to be that kind of person who judged parents when their children were having a meltdown within ten feet of me. My mother always had my sister and me under control. I hardly ever melted down in public with my mother, because I knew there would be a slap-slap-slap of the *chinela* when we got home.

But I was raising a child in the 2000's in America, where corporal punishment was/is frowned upon. So I gave up. And I said, "Okay…okay…*sh-sh-shhh*, CJ. You can stay in the car."

He started to calm down and made a hiccup sound as he settled down.

Thank God, he stopped screaming. I grabbed the handle bar again and hoisted my entire weight to get the cart rolling.

I managed to fit the cart through the automatic sliding doors, which in retrospect, are not wide enough for these carts in my opinion.

We headed down the dairy aisle going in a straight line, and the cart developed a little momentum. But when I had to stop to get to the milk, the cart was too heavy. So I kind of leaned back and stuck my butt out at the same time, trying to create a counterbalance to stop the cart. It worked. *Whew!*

Then I threw my weight into pushing the cart once again to get it going. And it got going, all right. It picked up a little too much momentum.

I reached the end of the aisle by the meats and freezer section and needed to turn right toward the produce section. There was no way to turn left anyway. But the cart was rolling on its own, and I realized I needed to slow it down enough to make the turn.

You know how truck drivers have to steer the big trucks wide before they can make a turn in order to avoid clipping the corner? That's what I was going to have to do with this thing.

So I steered the cart a little to the left and pushed with my left arm to make it go right. I got the cart to go right, but the momentum was too much. As it rounded the corner, it slew me to the left and sent me slamming into a display of Little Debbies. I knocked the boxes in every direction. The cart crashed right into the freezer end cap and came to a stop.

CJ was saying, "Wee! Wee! Wee! Car! Car!" with a gurgling toddler laugh.

The guy behind the seafood counter saw the whole thing go down, and he came out from the back. "Ma'am, are you okay? Do you need help?"

I was on the verge of tears and said, "I'm fine. My baby!"

"He's okay. The freezer stopped the cart."

I frantically grabbed at the Little Debbie boxes and tried to restack them on the table. "Oh, I'm so sorry!" The boxes kept falling off the table and onto the floor like an unstoppable cascade of sugary treats, and Little Debbie's dimpled face on the boxes just mocked me. It was the worst day ever. I said again, "Oh, I'm so sorry!"

"Ma'am, it's okay. We'll get this."

"No, let me help. I made the mess." Another box fell to the floor, and that one box was the straw that broke the camel's back.

I had not slept in two years. Motherhood just caught up with me right at that very moment, and I burst into tears. Right there in the freezer section between the breakfast sausages and the Little Debbies, I started to cry uncontrollably.

"Ma'am. It's okay, really we can clean this up. Are you okay?!"

Through my streaming tears, I said to the store clerk, "I'm so damned tired! I just want to get some milk and fruit! And I need a nap so bad! I just want to go home!"

"Well, ma'am, do you want me to get the milk and fruit for you?"

"No, I don't know what kind of fruit anymore! I…(sniff)…I (sniff)…I just…(sniff) I just want to go home…(sniff)…I'll send my husband to the store later. Can you help me get this cart out to the garage?"

"Yes, of course. It'll be alright. You'll be able to sleep again. I have three kids, I remember what it was like when they were little."

I fished a burp cloth out of the diaper bag and used it to wipe my tears.

"Thank you. You're very kind. I'm so embarrassed." People were starting to stare.

I did not get his name, and I wish I had. He helped me get to my car and he pushed the cart all the way. One of the reasons I like Publix so much is because they will help you load groceries to your car, and in this case, no groceries, but a baby and a diaper bag.

I'm sure a lot of people were entertained that afternoon.

CJ is eleven years old now, and I don't have to push him around in the cart anymore. Pretty soon, he'll be old enough to send to the store. But then how will I get my weekly dose of humanity?

That Midtown Publix is the most interesting. I mentioned it was the store for most of the Georgia Tech students.

One day not so long ago, I was at that store on a Saturday afternoon. I normally try to avoid grocery shopping on a weekend afternoon, because that is when the whole world is at the store. But in that case, my day's schedule was thrown off by a flat tire, and if I didn't go grocery shopping then, it wouldn't get done.

There were a lot of students shopping that afternoon. I suddenly had the realization that all the students were new to "adulting."

There was a group of four of boys wearing Georgia Tech shirts, long athletic shorts, and sneakers. They were tag teaming with one grocery cart between them, and they had a group leader. The team leader was super bossy. He had the master grocery list and was barking orders at the other three. Using his pointer finger, he said, "You, get the marinara sauce and pasta! You, get the ground beef!"

Then he says to the last person, "You and me, we'll go on the hunt for the garlic bread!"

At first I thought, "Is this a game they are playing? Are they on a scavenger hunt?"

I skirted around them in that same dairy aisle where I lost control of a cart with a baby nine years earlier and said, "Um, excuse me." They didn't hear me.

So I said it again a little bit louder, "Um, hey guys. Excuse me, may I get by?"

The team leader says, "Oh! Guys! Back up! Back up! Outta-the-way!"

At that point I realized that this was not a game they were playing. They were literally just grocery shopping. So I decided to say something to them using my soothing maternal voice I normally use for CJ when he is having a meltdown.

"Guys, relax. It's just grocery shopping. Just go down every aisle and check things off your list. It won't take that long. This store isn't big like Costco."

One of them took a deep breath and said, "Oh, ma'am, thank you! I normally go to the store with my mom or dad, but never by myself!"

I thought math and reading test scores were the most important thing for students, but this made me think we need to bring Home Ec classes into the classrooms again. Young people need life skills to survive everyday life.

"You're welcome. And when you get to the checkout line, be sure to use one of those plastic dividers so your groceries don't get mixed up with someone else's. And tell the cashier up front you want to split tender the bill four ways, and he or she can do that."

"Really?! Cool! Thanks!"

"You're welcome guys! Good luck!"

And with that, I pushed my little cart by them and made a right toward the produce section. About thirty minutes later, I saw them in the checkout line. I pulled up right behind them. They used the plastic divider. I heard the team leader say to the cashier, "We would like to split tender the bill four ways, please."

The corners of my mouth slid up into a little smile, and I felt pretty good about myself for helping four newly minted young adults learn how to be adults.

Kindness at the Publix happens often. At the Ponce Publix, there is an older cashier named Miss Betty. Miss Betty and I have become great friends. Whenever I go to that store I always look for her, and I make sure I get in her line.

One Friday during mid-afternoon, rush hour at the grocery

store hadn't quite started yet. I got my weekend grocery shopping done fairly quickly and found Miss Betty's checkout lane. As usual, she was at cash register six or seven, toward the middle of the row. She saw me and perked right up, "Well! Hello, darlin'!"

Miss Betty came around from behind the cash register. I met her in the aisle, and we put our arms around each other.

"Hello! Miss Betty, how you doin'?!"

"Oh, baby, I'm not too good these days."

I furrowed my brow. "Why, Miss Betty? Are you okay?"

"Well, I may have to move out of my apartment."

I put my hand on her arm and asked, "Why?"

"I'm not sure I can afford it anymore. I may have to move in with my sister."

"Well, would that be so bad if you moved in with your sister?"

"Nah, we get along all right. But I do wish I could get just a few more hours. It would help to have just a little more money."

"Yes, just a little more money is always a good thing."

Miss Betty went back around to the register, and I unpacked my cart. The conveyor belt moves, and she takes the Lunchables and rotates each one to the bar code. Beep...beep...beep... beep.

"Miss Betty, I will pray for you and hope it all works out."

"Yes, honey. I can use all the prayers I can get."

She scanned the last item, and the bagger loaded up my cart. I use my debit card passcode and the credit card machine reads "Remove Card." I pull out my card and the long grocery receipt begins to print out.

"Okay, Miss Betty, you take care and I will see you next week."

She hands me my receipt and I fold it and shove it into one of the grocery bags.

She says, "Have a great weekend!"

The grocery bagger says, "Ma'am do you want help to your car?"

"No, thank you. I've got it."

He nods and turns his attention back to the new set of grocery items coming off the conveyor belt.

I grabbed the handlebar of the cart and made my way out of the store, deep in thought about Miss Betty.

She looks to be in her mid-sixties. I ventured to guess she is probably collecting some kind of Social Security check by now and has probably qualified for Medicare a few years ago. She is probably mostly on a fixed income and working at the grocery store to make ends meet.

I also thought that no matter what happened, she will probably eventually have to move in with her sister, because rent in Atlanta is on a fast trajectory to getting steeper and steeper.

As I unpacked the last bag into the car, I thought about my mother. I thought of how much of a blue-collar worker she was and how she carefully managed her finances. She always provided for my sister and me. We were never hungry, and we were always properly clothed. But it was hard. There was not a lot of extra money for frivolous things. When we went shopping, it was always with a list. Miss Betty and my mother had a lot in common.

Then I made up my mind. Once I was in the car, I reached into my purse and got out my phone while I was still parked.

I put my finger on the Google Chrome icon and searched for "Publix Ponce de Leon."

I found the right location and punched the "Call" icon.

I navigated the automated system and got a person on the line, then requested a manager.

"This is Bob, how can I help you?"

"Hi, Bob. My name is Maria, and I'm that really tiny Asian woman who shops there."

"Oh, yes, ma'am. What can I do for you?"

"I'm calling about Miss Betty."

"Is everything all right?"

"Yes. Nothing is wrong. It's just...well, I was wondering if you had any control about scheduling for the staff."

"No ma'am. One of the other managers does that. Is there something I can assist you with?"

"I was wondering if you all would consider giving Miss Betty a few more hours a week. She's one of your best cashiers, and she's been there a very long time. She's always great with the customers."

"Yes, ma'am, we do like Miss Betty. I'm not sure if we can give her more hours."

"Well, could you just mention it to the other manager so they can consider it?"

"I can mention it, but we can't make any promises. And we have other people who need hours, too."

"Yes, I understand. If you could just mention it, it would be great. I appreciate you not saying 'no,' right away."

Saying "no" to me can be a difficult thing. I usually take a "no" as "No, not right now. Maybe later."

"Okay, ma'am. I'll mention it. Have a good day."

"Thank you. You have a good day, too."

I hung up and started my car, and I sighed deeply. I'm not sure why I felt so relieved, but I did. It's just that a social worker took a chance on my mother many years ago when she walked into a senior center looking for a job. That social worker put in a good word for my mother and got her a job which opened up so many doors for my family. I often feel compelled to pay this forward. Even if they give Miss Betty four extra hours a week, that would be about $40 extra dollars for her. That could be a prescription co-pay or groceries for her.

I don't know if my phone call ever went anywhere and if they gave her more hours, but she still works there and she still flashes her warm smile at me. Sometimes the line for her lane will be the longest, and I don't care. I will still get in her line. Interaction with her is worth the extra time.

CHAPTER 12

The Friends at the Bar

As a single, middle-aged woman living in a big city like Atlanta, I have no excuse to sit at home, unless I choose to. There are plenty of events around town, plenty of good restaurants and plenty of good bars.

I frequent about three places regularly: The Pinewood in Decatur, Frogs in Midtown, and Murphy's in Virginia Highlands. You will probably find me there on any given Tuesday, Wednesday or Thursday, which are the days I do not have custody of my son. All these places are also along the six mile stretch between my house and work.

Having regular places means I have developed great friendships. I will go to these places, depending on which group of friends I want to see and what kind of mood I'm in for food and drink.

The best part about having several places to hang out in is the diversity of my friends. For example, I go to Frogs in Midtown because this is where a lot of my gay friends go. And the best lesbian bartender in Atlanta, Twee, works there. She's the one who got me hooked on that place. She is one of my favorite people in town. She's funny, kind, good at her job, and is always "keepin' it real." Frogs is not a fancy place. It has good Tex-Mex food and awesome margaritas. It's a brightly decorated place in the same shopping center as the Midtown Trader Joe's and located across the street from Grady High School off Monroe Drive. The bar itself is a mosaic tile in a big "L" shape with wooden stools, and you can see into the kitchen from the bar.

My favorite part about Frogs other than the people and food is a small piece of concrete on the liquor shelf that's labeled "Murder Kroger."

About twenty years ago, there was a tragic murder that occurred in the Kroger on Ponce de Leon Ave. in Midtown. People started calling it "Murder Kroger." The supermarket chain and new developers have been trying to shake the name ever since and have tried to rename it "Beltline Kroger." But we older locals won't have it. It will forever be Murder Kroger. We have a tendency to nickname things in the south, especially our supermarkets, and it will be two generations before the name will change, except for street signs. For some reason those change frequently. I will withhold my personal feelings about that ("fixing my face" right now). Murder Kroger is torn down now, and they built a bougie Kroger off the Beltline path on the East side trail. I guess they got what they wanted.

So I go to Frogs to see my gay friends. If you are a smart, put-together woman in Atlanta, you better have gay friends. The LGBTQ are strong in Atlanta. I go to Frogs to socialize and have great conversation. But I also go prepared with selfie photos of myself in various outfits I am planning to wear for upcoming occasions. Yes, I do this. Shut up.

At the bar, I will scroll through the "Fashionista" album in my phone, and my Frogs friends will give me feedback, "No, honey, that hem is too long for you. Take it up a little." Or, "Yaaass! Wear that!"

It's not just the fashion advice. It's financial advice too. They know real estate in Atlanta. If you want to see the next up and coming neighborhood in the region, look for the rainbow flags on porches.

But my gay friends at this bar are older and they give me a strong sense of the past for their community. Many of them lost friends to AIDS, and you can see the heartache in their eyes when they recall that difficult time in the 80s. I connect with these friends, because I have been through my own identity crisis after finding out I was adopted. I know what it feels like to be questioning who I am and where I belong. I'm not purporting that I know what it's like to be LGBTQ. That's like saying I know what it's like to be black. I don't. I'm just saying I can relate, sympathize and connect. It turns out there is a letter assigned for people like me in the LGBTQ community. I'm an "A" for "Ally."

I am especially known for hanging out at The Pinewood in Decatur. The staff there refer to me as "The Regular." There is a craft cocktail named "The Maria." It's not on the printed menu anymore, but it is in their bar book and you can still request it.

Good bartenders to me are alchemists, not just bartenders. They memorize dozens of recipes with ingredients and precise measurements. If you think shaking a drink is just shaking a metal can, then you are wrong. There is a right way and a wrong way to shake a drink. A good bartender will plant his or her feet firmly and shake from the core of the torso. If they shake with their arm, they will have a rotator cuff injury in no time. In addition to good physical form, all five of their taste centers have to be on point. A drink can be too sour, too bitter, or too watered down by too much ice in the shaker. They are modern day alchemists, I tell ya.

The Pinewood in Decatur, of course, has a beautiful wood bar with tall metal stools. It's located on the corner of W.

Ponce de Leon Avenue and Ponce de Leon Place, across the street from a CVS shopping center in downtown Decatur. It is about three blocks west of the old Decatur Square. The interior is soothing to me. The walls are a light bluish gray with ecru wainscoting. There are very bright and open windows on the front of the bar, and usually a bouquet of fresh flowers on the hostess stand by the front door.

A year ago, on a slow Tuesday night, the former bar manager, Jay, said, "Hey, Maria, let's make up a cocktail."

Jay was the quintessential hipster Millennial with a plaid shirt, jeans, and a very long beard. Jay and I would have long discussions about Malcolm Gladwell books. I love Gladwell, but Jay did not. He always felt Gladwell was contrite, whereas, I felt Gladwell shapes my thinking. Which he does.

"Yes! Let's do that! You know I love B&Bs and scotch. Can we do something with those two things?"

He thinks a moment, and says, "Oh, man, that would be a very boozy drink."

"Well, yes, of course."

"Let's play around."

Jay put a mixing glass on the bar on top of a blue and white napkin folded long ways. He put a rocks glass next to the mixing glass. He got liquor bottles from the middle shelf—no bottom shelf for me! He started using the jigger on both ends, measuring and pouring into the mixing glass, then stirred for about 20 seconds. Then he poured some Laphroaig 10 scotch into the rocks glass, swirled it around in the glass and then dumped it. That's called a rinse, not alcohol abuse. You might disagree. Then he scooped exactly four ice cubes and put it into the rocks glass, and then poured the mixed cocktail into it. Then he used the peeler to strip an orange and twisted the orange zest over the drink before dropping it into the glass.

This is called "The Maria" and has a Laphroaig 10 scotch

rinse for the smoke and peat, Great King Street scotch, cognac, an orange zest, and it's stirred, not shaken.

Oh, it's boozy, all right! Thank goodness for Uber.

Whisky, or the general category of spirits, is not just a social lubricant. Spirits should be consumed for taste and for relating with other people. When you sip a good whisky, you relax and talk to people, or you think and broaden your mind and feelings. And if you are smart, you pair the spirit with good food. Good, smoky peaty scotches such as Lagavulun 16 or Oban 14 (my favorite) are great with a medium rare grilled filet steak, garlic mashed potatoes, and sautéed asparagus or green beans with a little bit of olive oil and lemon zest. If you are not enjoying and tasting the spirits that have been distilled and aged for 10 years or more, then you might be missing out on something.

I was the keynote speaker at a whisky tasting
called "Spirited Women" in April 2019.

CHAPTER 13

The Idiots on Scooters

I live in the heart of Atlanta in a neighborhood called Centennial Place. It is situated in the midst of both Georgia State University and Georgia Institute of Technology. There are students everywhere.

Centennial Place used to be called Techwood Homes, one of the first housing projects in the U.S. It was completed in 1936. It's considered a historical neighborhood, and there is still a historical structure on the property that is on the U.S. National Register of Historic Places. When Atlanta won the Olympic bid in the 1990s, city leaders and developers decided to tear down Techwood Homes and rebuild new housing with multi-income tiers. It's one of the few places in the heart of the city where people in lower income brackets can live in good, decent affordable housing. The developer, Integral, didn't just tackle the affordable housing issue. It also tackled the education issue and helped to establish a charter school called Centennial Academy Charter School. The CEO of the company is a well-known leader in Atlanta named Egbert Perry. Egbert is one of that different breed of leaders in this world who are visionaries. He had a vision for Centennial. He wanted to create a community inclusive of all people—young students, seniors, people of different races, and different incomes. I once heard him say at a speaking engagement, "Why can't children with dark skin be able to live in a good, safe neighborhood with a good school?"

I totally agree. My son, CJ, goes to this school, and he has been there since Kindergarten. The kids at Centennial come from varying socio-economic backgrounds, and there are many children of color. I really want my son to be exposed to people who are different from him, so that he is comfortable with people from diverse races, religion, and backgrounds. It is important to me that my son internalize all people and for him to be comfortable with being mixed race—being half Asian and half white.

In addition to being so close to Centennial Park and Pemberton Square, where the Georgia Aquarium, the Center for Civil and Human Rights Museum and the Children's Museum are located, the Coca-Cola Headquarters is directly adjacent to the development. When I sit on my back patio, I look right at the Coca-Cola tower, with its bright red script. The Coca-Cola Company built Atlanta. I am deeply loyal to Coke. When we hosted Super Bowl LIII in Atlanta, Pepsi was a major sponsor. Ads for Pepsi started going up in downtown and in train stations. I was just beside myself and felt frustrated, invaded, and oppressed! For most people, the Super Bowl was one weekend, but for me, who lives in the heart of the city, it was one week. But on the night of the Super Bowl, I tuned in to watch from my living room. The coin toss included our civil rights leaders, Congressman John Lewis, Ambassador Andrew Young, and Bernice King, Martin Luther King Jr.'s youngest daughter. My feelings about the Super Bowl changed from frustration and anxiety to pride. I got emotional and realized how proud I was that our city was hosting another big sporting event.

Atlanta is the cradle of the civil rights movement in America. That topic has its own books. It's a deep part of our culture and identity. To see our civil rights leaders doing the coin toss was quite moving. I will reserve my opinion about how unmoving that game was, however.

Atlanta is one of the fastest growing regions with over 4.6 million people in a ten-county area. Traffic in Atlanta is legendary. I suppose this is what makes this market so attractive to alternate transportation companies like Uber, Lyft, and e-scooter companies.

First, let me state that I do believe in last mile connectivity, especially for people who do not have cars. You have to remember that I am an immigrant whose mother did not have a car and worked as a housekeeper in Chattanooga, TN for almost thirty years. We relied on public transportation and rode the CARTA buses in Chattanooga until my mother was finally able to learn to drive and afford to buy a car.

So I am fully aware of the necessities of public transit and last mile connectivity. That being said, I do rant about the e-scooters and how they entered the marketplace. My neighborhood is right by a university, so it is prime real estate for e-scooters. Imagine coming home from work one day, and right there on sidewalks are rows upon rows of e-scooters. I don't recall seeing any public notices that they would appear. I don't recall any public policy hearings or town hall meetings to draft ordinances or legislation for them being on public right of ways that were built and paid for by taxpayer dollars. As a voting member of the population, I don't remember being asked if they could use our sidewalks and roads.

Sometimes, they are not even in perfect rows. Sometimes, they are lying across the entire sidewalk, making it hard for people to walk and making it hard for anyone in a wheelchair. And what about visually impaired people? What if they trip over one of those things? I am not disabled in any way, and I have almost tripped over one. I almost ran over one with my car because it was left strewn in the middle of the street.

But the hardware is only half the problem. The majority of the problem in my opinion is that these things are readily available to just anyone with a credit card and a few bucks to spare to go a few blocks. Just because you have a credit card and a few bucks to spare does not mean you have the skills to balance and ride these things. There's no test for a license to ride them. There's no measure for how much a rider understands the rules of the road, and in fact, when they first entered the marketplace, there were no rules. The city has struggled to respond and draft ordinances to protect everyone and to do so quickly. What about this argument that we need more bike lanes for scooters and bikes? Yes, I agree. But it takes time to build that infrastructure, and forcing the change on the public and putting lives at risk in the meantime is not the answer.

There are about twenty-five scooter accidents per month reported at the emergency room at Grady Memorial Hospital. An injury can be anything from a few bruises to a severe fracture or break. The medical cost can be anywhere from a $500 co-pay to $10,000 in medical bills along with rehabilitation. In a country where we are struggling with health care and health care costs, is this how we want to solve the last mile connectivity issue? That injured person might have had a few bucks to go a few blocks on the scooter, but do they have thousands of dollars for medical bills if they get injured, and who is liable? The rider. The waiver is locked down tight and protects the scooter companies.

And these things are fast.

When you combine heavy traffic, pedestrian traffic, and now people without helmets on scooters going fifteen miles per hour, it's a dangerous cocktail. At the time I am writing this book, there have been four fatalities reported in Atlanta. Four is too many. One is too many.

I have seen students riding around on these things while on their phones. It makes me want to get out of my car and yell at them like I'm their mother.

So it's not the scooters per se, it's the idiots on scooters that drive me insane.

There's an entire category of physics called Newton's Laws of Motion. One of the principles is a scientific Law of Conservation of Momentum. Basically, this law of physics says there is a direct correlation between the mass of an object, its speed, and its ability to stop. So if I am in a two ton car going thirty miles an hour and I have to brake fast and hard, it does not mean my car will stop on a dime. I could be putting all my body weight on the brake and my car will still not stop.

This principle was really put to the test one spring day when I was on my way to work. I was driving the speed limit on Centennial Olympic Park Drive and was approaching the intersection of Centennial and North Avenue. This intersection is across the street from the Georgia Tech football stadium and the student dining hall. There are students everywhere, and they are on scooters. A student was going west at full speed on the sidewalk on North Avenue, and I was in the right lane on Centennial about to turn right onto North Avenue. I had the green arrow, but this student did not look to see that I had the arrow and apparently didn't care.

I slammed on the brakes, and I'm pretty sure I burned rubber. That kid zipped right in front of me, looked over his shoulder, and shot me an "eat shit" look.

He had a warped sense of security, because he did not know the law of physics. He forgot he was in human skin, and I was in a Honda CRV.

I felt angry and scared at the same time. I do not want to injure or kill anyone with my car. It's not like I got up that morning and said to myself, "I think I'll hit a scooter rider with my car today." No! But I felt angry at the same time, because he was an idiot. And then I felt angry, because we were letting this sort of thing happen.

But are we letting it happen, or is it happening *to* us? There are now ordinances that ban the scooters in Atlanta at night, and riders are not supposed to ride on the sidewalks. So now the scooter riders have to share the road with cars. That's no better.

There are 2,000 sworn police officers in Atlanta. There are half a million people who actually live in the city limits, but on any given day, when there are students and workers who commute into the city, that population goes up significantly. So, who is going to enforce all these rules? The 2,000 police officers have their hands full. They are dealing with real crime in some areas of Atlanta. Do they really have time to cite a yoga-mat-toting-Lululemon-wearing-hipster riding a scooter illegally on the sidewalk?

Looking back on that "eat shit" look, it drives me crazy. Crazy! The worst is when this happens, and I'm in the middle of a hot flash. Then it's just over for me. I just go home and scream into a pillow, and say to myself, "Maria, tomorrow is another day."

CHAPTER 14

The Shamans in Leadership

The recession was at its peak in 2009. I took the layoff package from Troutman Sanders and started my own consulting business on a prayer. I knew that finding a new job was probably not going to be easy and that it would be easier to leverage my network securing projects here and there to piece together a monthly income. It was a financially difficult time, and I'm sure not just for me, but for many Americans.

There is a long list of people who helped me during this time, including friends who gave me office space so I had a place to go every day so I could be more professional and not feel like I was working in my bath robe in my dining room. Most importantly, this helped me not to feel isolated as an independent consultant. One of my offices was near West Peachtree Street and North Avenue. It was across the street from CJ's daycare at All Saints Episcopal Church and the North Avenue MARTA Station. Then I moved to Peachtree Walk and 13th Street in Midtown, behind the Four Seasons

Hotel. Both locations were in Midtown. I had my consulting business from 2009-2013.

My client list was diverse. I had nonprofit clients, corporations, and political candidates. It was hard work to generate projects and potential clients in the pipeline while at the same time, executing the work. I was a one woman show. On top of all that, I had a toddler and a quickly declining mother. CJ was a baby, my mother started to decline in 2009, and my sister had just passed away. I had a lot going on emotionally. At the same time, the timing for being an independent consultant was perfect.

I set my own hours and worked whenever I wanted to, unless I had an event with a client. This afforded me the opportunity to travel to Chattanooga to see my mother every week and take care of her. Mom developed dementia after my sister's death. It was never concluded that it was Alzheimer's, and looking back on it, the scientific determination only matters to me in that with dementia, Mom suffered longer than an Alzheimer's sufferer would have. This is a deep sadness in my life. My mother's illness dragged on for eleven years. I know God has a plan, but sometimes I feel He can be cruel and unfair. I sometimes feel mad at God about my mother. She was a loyal servant to Him.

I transitioned her from her two-bedroom house to a one-bedroom care facility in Chattanooga, then relocated her from Chattanooga to Atlanta, to a one room personal care home, and then a nursing home in DeKalb County, not far from the School District's Administration Offices. Do you know what it is like to pack up a person's entire life of seventy-plus years in just a few months and consolidate their entire existence to just a few boxes? Or what it is like to watch a person lose sense of themselves and see the light in their eyes slowly fade? I don't know when my mother stopped recognizing me, or if she never stopped recognizing me, because when I went to see her, she smiled. She always smiled. Every day, I pray that she is at peace. I used to tell the health care workers who cared for her, "Max out the meds and make sure she is comfortable at all times." I had to say such words for my dying sister and I said such words for my dying mother. It's a lot.

When I visited her, I tried to come during the mealtimes so I can see if she was getting nutrition. I sniffed her and made sure she didn't smell and they were bathing her and grooming her. My visits to her were difficult in that I had to make sure my head was in the right place, because it was so hard to see my mother so declined. The visits were not long. They were a matter of minutes, because Mom could no longer engage and carry on a conversation. She just wanted to sleep. But the impact on me were for days. The grief and the mourning were a constant presence.

My years consulting were difficult financial times, but in fact, it was the perfect timing to allow me to care for my mother before I moved her to Atlanta.

In the summer of 2012, I was well ensconced at offices in Midtown Atlanta. The offices were located next door to Pasta di Pulcinella and were old houses re-zoned for office space. There were three floors. Loft offices were upstairs, and lower level offices were on the basement floors. My little office, and the conference room were on the second floor. The building had beautiful wood floors and was tastefully decorated. There were French doors on the front, of the building and the furniture was in incredibly good taste. My little office was just the right size. My desk was right under a high window with nine rectangle panes. I had two big filing cabinets filled with office supplies, files and a printer.

It was in this office on a particular day when I received a call on my cell phone.

"Hello, this is Maria."

"Hello, Maria. This is Arnie Silverman."

"Well, hello, Mr. Silverman."

"You know who I am?"

"I know your brother, Bob Silverman."

"Oh, I'm sorry! I'm much better looking than Bob!"

We both laughed. It was as if there was no ice to be broken.

"What can I do for you, Arnie?"

"Well, Ann Cramer told me I should call you. We are looking for an Executive Director for Leadership DeKalb. Would you consider interviewing for the position?"

First of all, when someone drops the name "Ann Cramer" in Atlanta, you drop whatever you're doing and listen intently. Ann is a pillar in the Atlanta community, and she knows everyone and everything. When Ann connects people to people, it is with good reason. So I knew Arnie wasn't bullshitting me the moment he dropped Ann's name.

My thoughts raced. I knew what leadership programs were, since I had graduated from Leadership Atlanta in 2006. Leadership programs help people engage in communities and become more informed about issues so they can be better leaders. In the case of the Leadership DeKalb Program, the topics covered are Integrity & Ethics, Diversity & Inclusion, History Arts & Culture, Government, Justice, Education, Health, and Economic Development. These are broad but key topics in every community. I have now been steeped in these subjects for the past seven years.

So I quickly said to Arnie, "Yes. That sounds interesting."

Arnie said, "Well, I know you have a consulting business that you like very much. Would you consider talking to me and to Bo Spalding, who is the incoming board chair?"

"Yes. I would be happy to talk with you and Bo."

"Let's meet for brunch this Saturday at 11:00 a.m. at Druid Hills Golf Club. I have a tee off at noon."

"Sounds good. See you then."

When I hung up the phone, I had a feeling. I had the sense that my life was about to change again. I immediately started Googling the organization and its board. I wanted to get the lay of the land.

I remember struggling about what to wear to a Saturday-brunch-semi-job-interview. It was July, so I settled on white slacks, a colorful top from Dillard's and sandals. My hair was long then, so I kept it down and didn't pin it up into a bun.

Druid Hills Golf Club is on Ponce de Leon and Clifton Road, near The Fernbank Museum of Natural History. It is in DeKalb County, but in the central part of the county and on the edge of the City of Atlanta. The approach to the club is that beautiful curved part of Ponce with lush tress and green grass.

We were seated in a roomy booth with leather seats. It was airy and bright with windows all around.

Arnie Silverman owns a construction project management company, and many construction projects in the region have a banner that say "Silverman Construction." Bo Spalding is a co-founder of one of the most prolific and successful communications company in the U.S. called Jackson Spalding.

But during that brunch, my first impression of these guys was not about how much they were men of industry and success. My first impression of them was that they were on the board of a small nonprofit in DeKalb that needed their help. They didn't at any time talk about themselves and their great success. They didn't at any time talk about how powerful or influential they were. I knew how influential they were because I had done my research and from simply being in the community for so long. But they didn't posture, and they didn't have a need to impress upon me who they were. I recall being a little surprised by this, but mostly, I was impressed and humbled to be in their presence. And that tone of humility would ring true for me in the years that followed.

I recalled what Sam had said to me many years earlier, "Look for the shamans in every workplace." Could Arnie and Bo have been shamans? Were they modern day healers of a tribe of people who communed with spirits and battled between good and evil? Were they wise men? Yes. Yes, they were. And I was about to meet a whole slew of shamans.

After that brunch, there was a very long waiting period. I did not hear back from them again until November of 2012. I thought that I had not gotten the job, or that they had found a better candidate or changed their minds. Whatever the reason, I made sure I didn't pester them and constantly follow up.

Arnie finally called me back in November. "Maria, hello, this is Arnie."

"Hello, Arnie. Happy holidays."

"Happy holidays. Are you still interested in Leadership DeKalb?"

"Yes. Are you all still interested in me?"

"Yes. We want you to interview again and meet the rest of the Board."

"Okay, sure."

"The meeting will be at my office."

"Sounds good. E-mail me the date and location. I'll be there with bells on."

"Will do. See you soon."

And with that, we hung up.

For the interview, I wore navy blue and cream, and I wore my hair in a low, tight bun with intricate hand painted hair chop sticks. I remember how grateful I was that I had had a good night's sleep. Tony took care of CJ the night before so I could be fresh for the interview.

I was nervous and excited at the same time. The interview

was bull-in-the-ring style, where they put me at one end of the conference room table and the board members were seated around in a U shape. They asked me questions in rapid fire. It was nerve wracking, hard, and exhilarating all at the same time. But I got the job.

After I got the job in November, my first duty was to meet the entire board at a board meeting in December of 2012. I officially started in January of 2013.

My first program day was Justice Day. Talk about baptism by fire. The first part of the day was in a courtroom. There was a prosecution and defense panel followed by the various judges and their court programs. My notion that the justice system was entirely punitive and out to get you was completely flipped upside down. I heard about justice reform programs and rehabilitative programs to help people get out of ensnarement of the legal system.

But the thing that hit me the hardest was when one of the prosecutors for the juvenile court system talked about what it was like to prosecute young people and what it was like to investigate children who were victims. She relayed a story about the first time she had to interview a victim as young as five years old. I cannot imagine that. My heart was breaking as she told this story. My next thought was, "How on earth can you go home and have a normal life after something like that?" *This was her job. She did this every day.* I'm a strong person, but I'm not sure I am as strong as she is. She is a mom, a daughter, and a wife. She has a beautiful family. She leads in this community in every way and she has worked in the domestic violence community for a long time. She taught me that domestic violence is not only a women's issue. Domestic violence happens to men and boys, and sadly to *children, to little babies.*

She is not alone working in this space. Every day, there are fire fighters, police officers, judges, and lawyers working to help people stay whole and be productive members of society. All of them are shamans, negotiating with the demons that plague the mentally ill or those who are depressed and angry. I think they spend more time being social workers than they do enforcing law and order.

But Justice Day in January of 2013 was not the real a-ha moment for me. The real a-ha happened months later.

The participants of the program in 2013 had a tough and disjointed year. They had the former Executive Director, an Interim Director, and then they got me. If I were in that class, I would have felt disjointed as well. Two of them approached me at the graduation ceremony. One of them was an editor for the *Atlanta Journal-Constitution*. Her name is Shawn. She said, "Maria, we would like to do a survey for our class and submit it to the organization so we can give you feedback on our experience."

I responded, "Sure. That would be fine with me. That kind of information would help us a lot." I meant it. Surveys and feedback are helpful and informative to me to this very day.

Two weeks later, Shawn called me at the office to let me know that she had received the surveys back from their cohort.

I said, "Oh, good."

"Well, yes. We had good participation on the survey. But..."

"But...what? Is everything okay?"

"Maria, some of it will be tough to read for you, I think. The survey was anonymous in order to give people the opportunity to be honest and candid, and they certainly were. They didn't hold back."

"Okay. Well, send it over and let me read it."

"Okay. Call me when you are done reading, and let's talk further."

"Yes, will do."

We hung up, and in about two minutes the survey came into my inbox.

I opened the survey link sent it to print on our big printer in the copy room. I got the printout, went into my office, and settled into my office chair to read the survey.

Shawn was right. It was difficult to read. Most of the comments were about the program, but also the difficulty in the change of leadership midstream for them.

I read the survey twice and I got a pen and began underlining the things that I knew I could change and impact. When I finished reading, I got up from my desk and got water from the water cooler. I wasn't thirsty, but I just needed to get up from my desk, take a few minutes to collect myself, and enjoy the sensation of cold water in my throat as I weighed the hot words of the survey.

Back at my desk, I dialed Shawn's office number. She had caller ID because she picked up on the second ring and said, "Maria, how are you?"

And I said, "Well, Shawn, there's nowhere to go but up!"

She laughed, and said, "Oh, Maria. What a great reaction! I agree!"

Then I asked her, "Do you mind if I send this to the Executive Committee?"

She said, "Really? You want to do that?"

"Yes. I feel it would be important for them to see the data. And it will help me make a case for some of the changes I think we need to make. I agree with just about everything they said in this survey. Some of the things are logistics which are out of our control, but most of it is programmatic."

Shawn says, "Well, the survey is for you, and what you decide to do with it is up to you."

"Okay, then I'll send it today."

And I did. I spent the next six years working on the issues stated on that survey, but also adding to it surveys every year.

The work has been incredibly fulfilling. I know I must seem like such a Pollyanna talking about shamans in the workplace, but this is my true existence. I have the greatest honor to work with people who truly want to make a difference every day. The people around me are true leaders. They are powerful and influential, but you would never know it if you just ran into them at the grocery store. They are humble, regular people. They have families like the rest of us. But in their day jobs, they are moving mountains. Don't get me wrong, there are disagreements and conflict among them too, but our standard is civil disagreement.

I want to end on a high note. I don't know what the future holds, but my present is wonderful. My son is growing and flourishing, and my work and my friends are vast and engaging.

I have seen sadness and tragedy, but more than that, I have joy. As my fiftieth birthday appears on the horizon, it has been cathartic and rewarding reflecting on my journey. I now look ahead and enthusiastically make room for the new stories and memories that will come in the future.

If you have been a part of my life for the first fifty years, thank you. Here's to the next fifty.

EPILOGUE

It's Thursday, July 2, 2020, and I just poured a whisky. It's Old Forester Kentucky Bourbon. For the past five months I've struggled with what to write for this Epilogue, because it's hard to write about a historic moment like COVID-19 while it is presently happening. Everyday changes. The death toll is now over 100,000 Americans, and it keeps going up and it's hard to know when it will end. The reason the previous chapters of this book were easier for me to write is because those events happened some time ago. I had distance and I was able to gain perspective. Tonight, I decided to let go of the notion that I will write about this when it is over, because we have no idea when it will be over, if ever.

The impact of COVID-19 reverberates to the deepest part of the human soul. It's as if someone reached into you and turned you inside out. It has forced a naturally gregarious society to isolate and quarantine for almost six months, and many have given up and are throwing caution to the wind and going out and socializing anyway. But honestly, I am not judging those people, because I understand the impulse.

Many of the places I talk about in the third section of this book no longer exist—like The Pinewood, for instance. The staff at The Pinewood were not only workers there. They were my friends and a big part of my social fabric. I saw The

Pinewood staff more than my own family sometimes. Now the space where The Pinewood was located is dark and covered up. It has been a grieving process.

The scooters disappeared for five months because they were not considered an essential business. However, as of July 1, 2020, some of them came back, because let's face it, people still need to get around even during a Pandemic.

There's so much to talk about regarding COVID-19—where to begin? How about the schools closing and all parents had to become teachers overnight? How about all the families that depended on the two meals per day provided by the schools? How about all the people who lost their jobs and had to file for unemployment? How about the health care disparities and the fact that this Pandemic is disproportionately killing underserved populations because they were already vulnerable to begin with? How about the people who are in domestic violence situations and now they do not have a job to go to or a school to go to for safe-haven? And so on.

There are the upsides, too. I don't want you to think I have lost all optimism. COVID-19 has brought families closer together. People have discovered or re-discovered themselves. People are going to parks and trails and enjoying nature. Everyone had to adapt and innovate. The word "pivot" is so overused, but it's the perfect word really. We're not out drinking and driving. We're at home "Zooming" and drinking, because "Zooming" is now a thing. Where I once wore dresses for work, I now wear "Zoom blouses" with yoga pants. And I have purchased a selfie light that illuminates me for video conferencing. I have new hobbies, like bird watching. I found bird feeders that attach to the railing of my patio and I installed two birdfeeders, two bird houses, and a bird bath. For two weeks there were no birds and I didn't think they would ever come. Then one day, there were house finches! I have a big picture window in my dining room where I can watch the birds all day. There are purple house finches, a pair of northern cardinals, a pair of mourning doves, a tufted titmouse, and sparrows. And I think I saw a grackle taking a bath the other day. Of course, I have a bird book, a bird poster, and a bird caller.

But the bird feeders don't just attract birds. They also attract squirrels. There is a tree right by my patio, and for weeks, I would watch the squirrels climb that tree and look longingly at the bird feeders. Then yesterday right in the middle of a Zoom meeting, I saw a dark shape move on the patio rail and there was the squirrel. My immediate reaction was to defend my bird feeders and my patio. I calmly excused myself from the Zoom, went downstairs and got a broom. I swung at that squirrel like bloody hell. It leapt from the rail and onto the tree. Then I straightened my Zoom blouse and went back to my meeting. I realize I cannot continue to fight the squirrel with a broom every day. But what's really funny is how many people are trying to convince me they are smart, cute and loveable animals. Who knew there was a "Team Squirrel?" I will learn to co-exist with them eventually, but for now, I need to dislike something. I've been in quarantine for five-months, I've gained 10 lbs. and I'm a little cranky. Allow me the brief luxury to hate the squirrel.

For months I have worked in my dining room. A few things about this…one, there's a three-foot space between the electric socket and my dining room table. So, for five months, I have been stepping over cords every time I walk to and from the kitchen and dining room. Second, I have been sitting on dining room chairs, and that's exactly what they are—chairs for dining, not for long hours of typing or Zooming. My lower back and right hip are a hot mess, and a massage during a Pandemic is out of the question. I can barely get a pedicure. I had plans to open our office on July 7, 2020, but the COVID-19 cases surged last week and I realized we will not go back to the office for the rest of the year.

That means I have to set-up a real home office. Sounds easy enough, right? WRONG. The room for my home office was CJ's playroom and workout room. There's no desk, no credenza, no office chair, no printer and copier, there's absolutely nothing that remotely resembles "workspace." It has a treadmill, a yoga mat, weights, two kid's couches, Legos, train sets, plastic swords, family photos, Spider-man and Batman posters, and all of CJ's early childhood.

I started looking at IKEA for affordable options, but the only thing that did for me was reinforce the fact that I do not have a man in my life. I don't have a truck. I have a Honda Fit. I can't load anything, I can't lift anything up a flight of stairs, and I certainly can't assemble anything. I don't even have a drill. I have a hammer, a few nails, and a screwdriver. I panicked and went to Rooms to Go. Only later did someone tell me that IKEA will also do all this, but when I drove to IKEA, it was packed, like cars around the block packed. No, thanks. I choose my health over Swedish furniture.

This is the summer of sacrifice for me and my 11 year-old boy. We had to part with many things and make hard choices about what to keep and what to let go in order to make room for my workspace. In a course of a week, we have completely dismantled his entire early childhood and we are consolidating him to his bedroom upstairs. The people who claimed the couch came tonight and moved the couch out of the room, leaving a very cavernous space and a couple of rubber balls which had rolled under the couch and a dead spider. I cleaned up the mess and I went upstairs and sat in my chair, and that's when a tsunami of tears washed over me. COVID-19 had taken its emotional toll and it was time for me to write the Epilogue.

Every single chapter of my book was a good two-hour cry.

Ugly cry. Why should that be any different for the Epilogue? I am fully aware of how blessed we are. We are blessed that I am still gainfully employed and can work from home. We are blessed to have the extra room downstairs. We are blessed that I can grocery shop every week. We are blessed. We are blessed. We are blessed.

But I will not minimize the deep impact COVID-19 has had on me. I worry about *everyone and everything, and all the time.*

Because of COVID-19, there is a new social distancing norm and culture occurring, and it's like giving birth. It's messy, ugly, and painful. For example, the Publix installed directional arrows in every aisle so that people can shop in an orderly manner while keeping six feet apart. But not everyone follows the arrows and this can be very telling about a person's political perspective about COVID-19. One day I was shopping and I witnessed a man and a woman in the snack aisle face-off with each other. One of them (I'm not sure who) refused to follow the arrows and the other felt it was inconsiderate and irresponsible. Their argument escalated into very loud yelling, until a store employee intervened. But situations like this are happening all over America. Many people feel these new rules are encroaching on their rights and that we are overacting and it's just a bad flu. Many people feel everyone should behave responsibly for the safety and well-being of others and that this is not just a bad flu. And now you can sometimes tell on which side of this argument people are on based on whether they are wearing a mask or following the arrows. For the record, I wear a mask, but I don't always follow the arrows. This has more to do with my spacial memory of the store and how I shop. Also, I am 99% a rule follower, but there's that 1% where I bend the rules a little.

I would be deeply remiss if I didn't write about one other

historic moment. On May 25, 2020, a black man named George Floyd was killed by a white police officer named Derek Chauvin in Minneapolis, MN. George Floyd was lying on his stomach, on the ground in handcuffs, and Officer Chauvin was kneeling on his neck and he knelt on his neck for 8 minutes and 46 seconds, eventually killing him. The whole thing was caught on video. When I first watched the video, I wanted to look away. I wanted to press the pause button on my phone. It was gut wrenching to watch another human being die a slow and painful death. And George Floyd wasn't just dying, he was begging for mercy and cried out for his mother. I made myself watch it because I needed to be reminded of what hate and racism looked like. I recall the sensation of widening my eyes and blinking rapidly to see the video through my tears. I felt my shallow breathing and my own effort to breathe just watching the video. I can only imagine what George Floyd was feeling. COVID-19 had already turned us inside out, but the murder of George Floyd took our raw open wounds and set it on fire. It ignited protests *globally*. It made Black people who were already fatigued feel beyond tired. What is more tired than fatigued? I don't know, and I don't think "resilient" is adequate to describe Black people for the past 400 years.

My good friend, Dr. Karcheik Sims-Alvarado, who is an author and Civil Rights historian said, "Black Lives Matter used to be a hashtag, but now it's a Movement." She's right.

My other good friend, Nathaniel Smith, CEO of Partnership for Southern Equity, said, "COVID-19 has eliminated all the distractions—no bars, no restaurants, no commuting to work, and now we can really see the hatred and racism clear as day." He's right too.

Like COVID-19, there's so much on this topic—where to begin? I cannot speak for everyone. I can only speak for myself.

And what I have to say is this: I am a person of color. I have experienced discrimination and racism myself, but none of my experiences have ever escalated to the point where I feared for my life. Black and Brown people fear for their life. To me, this is why it's called "Black Lives Matter" and not "People of Color's Lives Matter." Many people want to say, "All Lives Matter." Yes, all lives matter. No one is arguing that point. But not all lives are in danger due to racism like Black and Brown lives. This is my opinion, and this is my book. If you have a different opinion, go write your own book.

I also feel it's important to state that not all White people are racist. Many White people have been advocates, benefactors, allies, and real friends to people of color. There are many White people who are equally outraged about racism, and who are among the protestors now and in protests in the past. Many White people have forged paths for people of color to succeed. I know my wealthy, Southern grandparents did that for me. Others share this same story, like my good friend Terry. "Terry" is not her real name.

Last week, my friend Terry came over for dinner. Terry sat in my canary yellow sitting chair directly across from my sitting chair, which is an identical yellow chair. She relayed her story. She told me that when she was 17 years old, a White man, named Donald (that's not his real name either), gave her an internship. He trained her for management from day one. He eventually sent her to Arkansas to run his Midwest operation. When she got her graduate degree, her own father could not be at graduation for some reason, but Donald was there—in the front row of the auditorium. He was her mentor, father figure and champion. When it was time for her to move from Arkansas to Atlanta, Donald showed up with a trailer, packed up all her stuff and drove her to Atlanta. She was a successful executive by the time she was 25 years old, and it was because

Donald championed opportunities for her. And she in turn, worked hard.

Then Terry leaned on the left arm of the chair and she gazed at the floor. When she began to speak again, her voice cracked and tears began to stream down her face. She said, "These race riots for the past few weeks have been difficult for me." I offered the box of tissues on the coffee table. I have boxes of tissues all over the house. I am always prepared for an allergy attack, or to be overcome with emotions and need to wipe away tears. It's called menopause. We didn't say too many more words about why it was difficult for her, because I understood exactly what she was feeling. Big sweeping movements like the Black Lives Matter Movement are good because there is a ground swell of support for real change. But there are casualties. The Black Lives Matter Movement can cause some people to think that all White people are racists. It causes distrust and can sometimes create unnecessary tension. The White people who are allies might accidentally get lumped in with the racists because they look White. Casualties. I feel the same way about The Me Too Movement. Many good men got lumped in with bad men simply because they were men. In an ideal world, people would take a minute before judging another person. In an ideal world, I would be 5' 5" tall and 110 lbs. You get my meaning.

How shall I finally end this book? I want to end it on a high note. The year 2020 is a challenge like no other I have ever experienced in my entire life—and that includes murder hornets and Sahara Dessert dust plumes (oh, yeah, that happened too). But the year 2020 has forced me to be still. Do you know how hard it is for me to be still? Being still is amazing. Being still is a gift. I am watching every hair on my son's head grow. Every time he grows a centimeter, I see it. I watched two trees in my back patio go from bare branches, to buds, to lush green leaves. The spring of 2020 was one of the most beautiful springs I have ever seen and the cool 70-degree weather seemed to last forever. When I go for my long walks in the neighborhood, I take my time because I don't have to be anywhere except for wherever I am at that moment. 2020 is hard because all good things are not easy. I believe that whatever is on the other side of this thing will be worth the hardship.